S0-CBD-189

ENJOYING

THE

Journey

ENJOYING
THE
Journey

STEPS TO FINDING JOY NOW

JAIME THELER
with
DEBORAH TALMADGE

HORIZON PUBLISHERS
SPRINGVILLE, UTAH

© 2008 Jaime Theler and Deborah Talmadge

All rights reserved.

No part of this book may be reproduced in any form whatsoever, whether by graphic, visual, electronic, film, microfilm, tape recording, or any other means, without prior written permission of the publisher, except in the case of brief passages embodied in critical reviews and articles.

This is not an official publication of The Church of Jesus Christ of Latter-day Saints. The opinions and views expressed herein belong solely to the author and do not necessarily represent the opinions or views of Cedar Fort, Inc. Permission for the use of sources, graphics, and photos is also solely the responsibility of the author.

ISBN 13: 978-0-88290-839-7

Published by Horizon Publishers, an imprint of Cedar Fort, Inc.
2373 W. 700 S., Springville, UT, 84663
Distributed by Cedar Fort, Inc., www.cedarfort.com

LIBRARY OF CONGRESS CATALOGING-IN-PUBLICATION DATA

Theler, Jaime.
  Enjoying the journey / Jaime Theler with Deborah Talmadge.
    p. cm.
  Includes bibliographical references.
  ISBN 978-0-88290-839-7
  1. Joy—Religious aspects—Mormon Church. 2. Christian life—Mormon authors. I. Talmadge, Deborah. II. Title.
  BX8656.T44 2007
  248.4'89332—dc22
                                  2007045661

Cover design by Nicole Williams
Cover design © 2008 by Lyle Mortimer
Edited and typeset by Annaliese B. Cox

Printed in the United States of America

10 9 8 7 6 5 4 3 2 1

Printed on acid-free paper

Contents

Acknowledgments

We want to thank Jason, wonderful husband and invaluable reviewer, Grammy for always being there, and Duane Crowther, who gave us the encouragement and little "nudges" we needed to finish this book.

CHAPTER ONE

Finding the Path

A FEW YEARS AGO I was given the temporary assignment to serve dinner to the sisters in the stake before the general Relief Society meeting broadcast. I felt a little out of my element because I had not even attended Relief Society in years, having happily served in Primary since I first began going to a family ward. In addition, I was also new to this ward and stake and I didn't know anyone, not even the other sisters behind adjoining tables who were serving with me.

As I stood awkwardly in back of the long serving table, a little embarrassed by the garish "Serve with Love" apron—complete with an assortment of pink hearts both large and small—that I was asked to wear, I discovered I was much more comfortable with children than women. Safely separated by the table I stood behind, I watched the sisters greet each other fondly and sit down together, happily chatting. I not only felt like a fish out of water, but a fish out of water and in deep space.

I decided that I could just slip out after I helped clean up, so after a quick bite in the corner, I lingered and continued cleaning up long after the other servers had found seats in the chapel. I wouldn't feel quite so guilty leaving if all the work was done. The meeting had already started, and from the gym where I wiped tables I could hear the other women singing the opening hymn.

I really didn't intend to stay, and now I can't remember exactly why I turned into the chapel instead of heading out the door. I probably just decided that I might as well listen for a while since I was already there and, to be honest, at the very least it was a break from the kids. Unobtrusively

I found a seat in the back at the end of a row, comfortably distant from anyone else. And then, with my "Serve with Love" apron wadded in my lap, I had one of those hit-you-over-the-head spiritual moments.

Sheri L. Dew, then second counselor in the general Relief Society presidency, gave a rousing address about the importance of the women in the Church and the need for us to stand tall. I was struck particularly hard by these words: "For though some would portray us as dowdy and dominated rather than the dynamic, radiant women we are, no woman is more persuasive, no woman has greater influence for good, no woman is a more vibrant instrument in the hands of the Lord *than a woman of God who is thrilled to be who she is.*"[1]

I am afraid that the rest of the talks and songs of that meeting did not get my full attention. I was gripped by that powerful statement, which played again and again in my mind. As I reflected on it, I had to ask myself: Do I ever feel thrilled, excited, or ecstatic to be who I am? Do I find joy in being a daughter of God—right here, right now?

I came to the painful conclusion that while I often felt *content* to be an LDS woman, so much of my life was dictated by routine and habit that I rarely paused to rejoice in my divinity. And I had to admit to myself that even sometimes I merely felt resigned to be me. I realized that I did not truly rejoice in who I was. Like most of us, I looked forward to and planned on having joy once I made it back to Heavenly Father, but I just wasn't finding it on the way there.

Sheri Dew's statement is not limited to women. Men, youth, single adults, senior members, and children can be more dynamic, radiant, persuasive, influential, and vibrant instruments if they rejoice in who they are. But too many of us have a hard time finding genuine joy and enthusiasm in being righteous children of God. Often we do not enjoy the journey.

We all know people who are thrilled to be who they are and have joy right now. Others flock to them because their joy percolates into everything they do. Marie and Lowry Bishop are two such people who simply and unashamedly glow with joy. Their dedication and enthusiasm in doing the Lord's work is well known in my hometown. As long as I can remember, I have had no doubt they were genuinely happy to be members of the Church. They have a spark that draws others to them, and they may very well be the most loved members of their ward, their stake, and the mission fields in which they served. The Bishops are thrilled to be who they are, they have joy because of this, and their actions reflect it.

The joy we are talking about is often shown outwardly by enthusiasm in pursuit of righteous acts. President Spencer W. Kimball was well known for his gung-ho, nonstop approach to everything he did. He was asked repeatedly why he maintained a grueling pace, one that would have been hard for much younger men to maintain. Likewise, anyone who has had the opportunity to visit with President Hinckley or even listen to him speak would agree that he is thrilled to be a child of God doing the Lord's work. And stories abound about the vigor, vitality, and enthusiasm of Joseph Smith as he served God and his fellow man. Both the New Testament and the Book of Mormon record striking examples of similar excitement and drive in Paul, Alma, and the sons of Mosiah (as evidenced by their fourteen-year mission among the Lamanites).

Enthusiasm by itself, however, is generally short-lived. Many companies spend large amounts of money hiring motivational speakers to help their employees find the enthusiasm to go beyond the mundane, to set lofty goals, and then to strive to reach them. Unfortunately, it is not unusual for the effects to wear off so that companies must provide a regular stream of "pep talks" to maintain the enthusiasm. Apparently, this is a state of mind that is challenging to reach but even more difficult to sustain.

So what do people like the Bishops, President Kimball, President Hinckley, Joseph Smith, Paul, Alma, and the sons of Mosiah have that so many others don't? Think about it. Not only do these people maintain their enthusiasm, but they often do it in the face of great adversity, bitter persecution, and grueling schedules. The key is that their enthusiasm and joy flows from a spiritual font, not from profit margins, point spreads, recreational toys, and so forth. No motivational speaker can remotely match the vitality infused by the Holy Spirit.

Motivational speakers do, however, understand one important principle of enthusiasm—it is contagious and gains momentum as it is shared. Since all truth stems from Christ, it should come as no surprise that the Lord has asked his servants to let their light shine, to open their mouths and speak, giving every man a reason for the hope that is in them. Individuals like Joseph Smith and Paul understood this because they labored during their lives to share their joy, and the Lord accordingly blessed them with joy in the journey—during this life, not just joy at the final celestial destination. Ammon expressed these feelings to his brothers: "Therefore, let us glory, yea, we will glory in the Lord; yea, we will rejoice, for our joy is full" (Alma 26:16).

While I can more clearly write about this now, the answer was much more elusive when I started the search. All I knew was that I wanted—and was entitled to—more joy and happiness, but I wasn't sure in what shape the answer would come or where I would find it. So, I began investigating different ways to accomplish this. It soon became obvious from the hundreds of available suggestions that I was not the only one searching for more happiness and joy. Some sources focused on self-esteem, giving me advice ranging from extreme makeovers, to changing my self-talk, to devoting more time to pampering myself. I tried implementing some of the sensible advice—like thinking positively or writing in a gratitude journal. These strategies helped a bit but still fell short of producing the level of happiness I believed I should be feeling.

I wanted to rejoice as Ammon did. I wanted joy like he felt, but I was still struggling to find the answer in the middle of a torrent of suggestions. Finally, and mercifully, I was reminded of the actions of young Joseph Smith who, like me, was confused and buffeted by the confusion raging around him. He read the scripture, "If any of you lack wisdom, let him ask of God, that giveth to all men liberally, and upbraideth not; and it shall be given him" (James 1:5). In his history, Joseph wrote, "I reflected on it again and again, knowing that if any person needed wisdom from God, I did; for how to act I did not know" (JS—H 1:12).

And how to become a more enthusiastic, vibrant, righteous child of God who felt joy in being myself I did not know either. Joseph Smith turned to the divine source of all answers, and I realized I needed to as well.

In this book I share with you the answers the Lord has revealed to me about how to find a greater measure of joy and rejoice in being a child of God—for they are one and the same. I hope that in these pages you may find kernels of truth that will uplift and inspire you in your own quest to find joy in the journey.

NOTE

1. Sheri L. Dew, "Stand Tall and Stand Together," *Ensign*, Nov. 2000, 94; emphasis added.

CHAPTER TWO

The Pursuit of Happiness

AMERICANS HAVE ALWAYS BEEN enamored
with happiness. Even our Declaration of Independence states that we all
have certain unalienable rights; among them are "life, liberty and the pursuit of happiness." But according to the latest Pew Research Center survey
(conducted in the beginning of 2006), just one-third of adults in this
country say they're very happy. Interestingly, this number has remained
stable since Pew began tracking in 1972.[1] The increasing prosperity over
the last thirty-five years has not resulted in a corresponding increase in
happiness.

Everyone wants to be happy, and the field of psychology has jumped
on the "pursuit of happiness" bandwagon in the last ten years. Branching
in a new direction, psychology was not satisfied with just fixing what is
wrong with people but wanted to study what "actively made people feel
fulfilled, engaged and meaningfully happy."[2] A fledgling branch of psychology, called positive psychology, has emerged as a result, and a flurry
of studies has been conducted on just what makes us happy.

Society tends to emphasize short-lived pleasure as the path to happiness, but the conclusions of positive psychology's research contradict
many of the common pursuits of happiness, most notably beauty, money,
and status. Martin E. P. Seligman, PhD, founder of positive psychology
and author of the book *Authentic Happiness*, contends that simply having
positive feelings will not produce enduring happiness. Greater happiness
comes when we feel *entitled* to our positive feelings, and that only comes
through the exercising of personal strengths and virtues.[3] Yet we have

invented myriad shortcuts to feeling good, and often these are the only pathways to happiness that people pursue.

As a result of his research, Seligman identifies three components of happiness: pleasure, meaningful relationships, and using personal strengths for a larger end. Of the three, pleasure is the least consequential. Interestingly, so many build their lives around pursuing pleasure when the other two components are much more important. Seligman writes, "Positive emotion alienated from the exercise of character leads to emptiness, to inauthenticity, to depression, and, as we age, to the gnawing realization that we are fidgeting until we die."[4]

We all have an inward pull or desire to be happy. Perhaps this springs from the spiritual knowledge that we gained—but can't remember—while we lived in our Eternal Father's presence and could see the joy that might be ours. An echo of that knowledge resonates in every one of us. It draws us to the divine and prompts an eternal pursuit of happiness and joy.

Satan knows of this divine spark and successfully leads many astray by promoting counterfeit happiness and obscuring true sources of joy. People think they will find happiness in following these false paths, but they never do. They cannot, because Satan has designed these sinister and sophisticated counterfeits so that it could be said of one generation after another: "But behold, your days of probation are past; ye have procrastinated the day of your salvation until it is everlastingly too late, and your destruction is made sure; yea, for ye have sought all the days of your lives for that which ye could not obtain; and ye have sought for happiness in doing iniquity, which thing is contrary to the nature of that righteousness which is in our great and Eternal Head" (Helaman 13:38).

According to Lehi, Satan fell from heaven, and in the process became "miserable forever." He, therefore, "sought also the misery of all mankind" (2 Nephi 2:18). Contrary to what some people may think, he is not trying to win the war that began in the premortal life. The outcome is predetermined. Satan's only aim is to inflict pain and misery on as many as possible. That includes both you and me.

In the Doctrine and Covenants the Lord gives us a glimpse into the pain and misery Satan will inflict. The latter days will be ones of strife and unrest, with wars and rumors of wars. The love of men shall wax cold with killing and fighting, and iniquity shall abound (D&C 45:26–27, 31–33). Peace shall be taken from the earth (D&C 1:35), all things shall be in commotion, and men's hearts shall fail them (D&C 88:91). We live in this prophesied time, and, though there are many temporal causes of commotion, Elder Dallin H. Oaks stated that an even greater cause of current commotion is spiritual.[7]

Paradoxically, many of those over whom Satan has power refuse to recognize he even exists. Nephi cautioned, "And behold, others he [Satan] flattereth away, and telleth them there is no hell; and he saith unto them: I am no devil, for there is none—and thus he whispereth in their ears, until he grasps them with his awful chains, from whence there is no deliverance" (2 Nephi 28:22).

Brigham Young University professor of ancient scripture Richard D. Draper warns:

> We must not be fooled into believing that there is some kind of neutral ground, that there are no absolutes, that we are free to "do our own thing." Such an attitude does not free us from Satan's grasp. Some people really do believe that they can do it their way, but if we watch closely, soon we will detect an emerging pattern. Those who do their own thing follow the same road as those who do Satan's. . . . They give up their chance at joy and exaltation without even sensing the decision. "Thus the devil cheateth their souls, and leadeth them away carefully down to hell" (2 Nephi 28:21).[8]

We need to understand and realize, in a very personal way, that we are constantly under attack. Elder Marion G. Romney warned, "There is a personal devil, and we had better believe it. He and a countless host of followers, seen and unseen, are exercising a controlling influence upon men and their affairs in our world today."[9]

The Lord's prophets have been pointing the way to true, authentic happiness since the beginning of time, and that is through obedience to his commandments. This should come as no surprise to anyone. Christ himself said of those who are obedient, "Well done, thou good and faithful servant: thou hast been faithful over a few things, I will make thee ruler over many things: enter thou into the joy of thy lord" (Matthew 25:21). Centuries ago, the Book of Mormon prophet Jacob counseled, "Hearken diligently unto me, and remember the words which I have spoken; and come unto the Holy One of Israel, and feast upon that which perisheth not, neither can be corrupted, and let your soul delight in fatness" (2 Nephi 9:51). And in this dispensation Joseph Smith reminded us, "And whoso is found a faithful, a just, and a wise steward shall enter into the joy of his Lord, and shall inherit eternal life" (D&C 51:19).

Unfortunately, it is alarmingly easy for worldly attitudes and viewpoints to creep into our lives and choke out our efforts to be obedient. The ideas that religion is restraining, that we can pursue personal endeavors at the expense of a family, or that gender roles are fluid are just some examples of attitudes that make it harder to be obedient. And we all know people (and likely have done it ourselves to a degree) who transgress a commandment and then look here and there for a way to be happy, while overlooking the one thing that would help them be happy. They change jobs, switch hobbies, swap relationships, or trade careers while continuing to disobey and then feel cheated because they aren't happy. Only through coming to Christ according to his terms and following the path he has outlined can we satisfy our hunger for lasting joy and happiness now and in the eternities. Then we can "delight in fatness" and rejoice in who we are. There are no shortcuts, and there is no other way.

It is important to note, however, that there are good, faithful people striving to come to Christ who nevertheless experience depression and despair. There are different kinds of adversities and trials: those that are common to mankind because we live in a fallen, imperfect world; those that are self-inflicted; and individual trials that Heavenly Father allows for our growth. Because of the emphasis placed on happiness as the reward of faithfulness, some may see their unhappiness as evidence of unworthiness. Furthermore, we read that "despair cometh because of iniquity" (Moroni 10:22). Understand that despair is part of our mortal experience (for some of us more than others), and that despair *does* come because of iniquity, but not necessarily *our own, personal iniquity.* Despair is a natural by-product of wickedness, and we live in a world rampant in wickedness.

You must understand that your level of happiness is not always and only a direct result of your faithfulness. If that were true, then Christ should not have experienced any unhappiness. Yet Isaiah describes him as "a man of sorrows, and acquainted with grief" (Isaiah 53:3). God the Father also feels sadness and weeps (Moses 7:28–29), so clearly even Godhood and perfection do not save us from sorrow. Ultimately, the source of our trials is not nearly as important as the way we deal with them.

LINE UPON LINE

Moving to another state for college was a big change in my life. I was facing many decisions that had greater impact on my future than I ever had before. Additionally, I was away from home and on my own for the first time. A few months into the school year, and overwhelmed by many things, I decided that it was time to get my patriarchal blessing. I needed a guiding hand to help me with big questions and very real concerns.

I did my best to prepare myself. I prayed, read my scriptures, and hoped for answers to specific questions that were troubling me and to which I couldn't seem to find the solutions. I traveled to my hometown on the appointed day and entered the modest home of the stake patriarch, my heart pounding in expectation. I just knew that I would finally get the answers I needed.

The patriarch laid his hands on my head and began to speak. I prepared myself for the direction and explanation I thought was coming. Before I knew it, the blessing concluded, without addressing a single one of the specific issues I had been praying about. I had thought that my blessing would be like an instruction manual, with specific guidance from my Heavenly Father. But all I had received was a few very general paragraphs.

I worked hard to quell my disappointment. The Lord knew me and what I had been expecting, so obviously I needed to work harder to find the direction I sought. Twelve years later, I realize the wisdom of the Lord in not giving me all the answers, but I sometimes find myself still wishing for step-by-step instructions.

Wouldn't it be nice to have such an instruction manual? When we are faced with challenges, we could just whip it out and flip to the page that would tell us exactly how Heavenly Father would have us handle incessantly quarreling children. Another day we could follow the detailed instructions on reviving a stagnant testimony, or the exact steps to ensure that our family is immune to materialism.

We are used to easily finding clear, detailed information. When I want to know how to get rid of mildew in the little overflow hole of my sink basin or identify the small animal leaving mounds of earth in my rock garden, I simply turn on the computer and in a matter of minutes I have half a million website hits to give me the information I need. As much as anyone, I like to have clear-cut directions and instructions, but I have learned that while character growth always requires faith, it is also usually accompanied by searching, struggling, and figuring things out on our own.

Many of us agree, at least intellectually, that true happiness and joy are found in spiritual matters and along spiritual paths. More difficult is internalizing the truth that there are no shortcuts in acquiring spiritual knowledge. Merely going through the motions will not give us joy. Doing what we are supposed to do and being where we are supposed to be can make us happier than we would otherwise be, much as a thirsty man is better off drinking a small amount of water than none at all; but our thirst for joy will not be quenched. Going through the motions prepares us to receive more happiness, but we will not have a fulness of joy unless we continue traveling along the spiritual path.

As an educator, my husband has been trained in different methods of instruction. One such method, called direct instruction, is where the teacher stands in front of the class and presents information. We have all experienced this way of teaching, and it has been a staple for many years, in many classrooms, and for many subjects.

Another method, one that is being used more and more, is known as inquiry based learning. It is rooted in the premise "tell me and I forget, show me and I remember, involve me and I understand." Rather than a teacher just dispensing information, this strategy involves students more in discovery, experimentation, and discussion scenarios. Inquiry based learning techniques often help students gain a deeper, more intuitive understanding of essential principles and content.

Inquiry based learning is more difficult than direct instruction for both the teacher and the student, requiring more preparation from the teacher and more effort from the student. It takes longer because students use exploration and analysis to internalize what is being taught in ways that make sense to them. This process not only takes time, but it also requires that learners take responsibility for their own learning and stick with the task.

Even though it is a longer, harder road, inquiry based learning can provide an experiential knowledge base that goes far beyond recall and regurgitation. However, you cannot do inquiry based learning all the time, nor can you do it without some background information, and direct instruction is an excellent method for introducing the requisite vocabulary and basic concepts.

In the gospel we receive a lot of direct instruction through the scriptures, general conference, and weekly church meetings. This instruction tells us the basic commandments and expectations of the Lord and gives us the rudimentary knowledge we need to experiment upon the word. But it is by experimenting, manipulating, and analyzing the word—like with inquiry based learning—that the principles we have tried and tested are incorporated into our character. And, like inquiry based learning, this takes time.

Alma highlighted some of the same principles that educators are taught in what many of us refer to as the "faith chapter" (Alma 32). Although I have read this section of scripture numerous times, I somehow missed the vital point that Alma wasn't just describing the method for gaining faith; he was telling us how to gain knowledge in all areas. You go through the same steps to believe in tithing, to develop faith in following the prophet, to accept and magnify a challenging calling, and, yes, to find more joy in your life.

The steps are (1) desire to believe, (2) make room in our hearts in order to experiment, (3) grow in belief, and finally (4) have knowledge. This may seem unexciting and tedious, especially for a fast-paced society, but there is no easy leap from doubt or so-so belief to deep knowledge and corresponding joy. Many people want to skip the seemingly slow spiritual method, and they subsequently lose out on profound spiritual knowledge and core-deep joy.

In his infinite mercy, the Lord has made the initial step in the process the easiest. At first we may only have a "desire to believe" (Alma 32:27). We can start by just *wanting* to be enthusiastic, joyful children of God—right now.

After we have a desire, we must "give place" (Alma 32:27) for the experiment. Elder Neal A. Maxwell stated, "This means giving place in our hearts, minds, schedules, and life-styles in order to make room to 'try the experiment of its goodness' (Alma 34:4)."[10] Just as we would research a large purchase like a car and test drive it before buying, we should "test drive" gospel principles.

By trying out a certain principle, or as Alma would say, nurturing the seed, we gain experience for ourselves. One way to test drive a principle is to live and act as if our knowledge was already sure and deep. As we do so, our faith in that thing will be strengthened as we practice it. Our belief will grow into confirmed faith, and, through time and testing, that faith grows into knowledge. Personal verification thereby occurs "in that thing" (Alma 32:34)—meaning, in the principle that is specifically obeyed and applied.

Other principles or doctrines need the same process of personal verification. We cannot "test drive" all gospel principles at once. We have to go through the process one at a time. Thus we learn, grow, and receive joy "line upon line" (D&C 98:12).

Alma did not say that you will never have doubts or be unsure about a gospel principle. Individual agency is a gift from God, and therefore it is not wrong to doubt or wonder about gospel matters. What matters is what we do about doubts when they arise in our hearts.

In the second chapter of 1 Nephi, Lehi made his family leave their home and possessions to travel in the wilderness for years, eventually settling in some promised land no one knew about—all of this based on a dream. Admittedly, this had to be hard for his family. When Laman and Lemuel had doubts about their father and his visions, they chose to murmur and rebel.

As 1 Nephi 2:16 shows, Nephi also had doubts, but he explained, "[The Lord] did soften my heart that I did believe all the words which had been spoken by my father, wherefore, I did not rebel." However, Nephi had a great desire "to know of the mysteries of God" and to know the truthfulness of what his father taught. He "did cry unto the Lord" until he received reassurance and had his faith confirmed (1 Nephi 2:16). Nephi followed the correct steps to acquiring spiritual knowledge. Once he earned that foundational knowledge and assurance, then he had the conviction and faith to follow his prophet father.

Just like Nephi and his older brothers chose the directions of their lives, we choose what we ultimately become. Elder Robert D. Hales said: "We have been given agency, we have been given the blessings of the priesthood, and we have been given the Light of Christ and the Holy Ghost *for a reason*. That reason is our growth and happiness in this world and eternal life in the world to come. . . . I testify that how we choose to *feel* and *think* and *act* every day is the way we get on the path, and stay on it, until we reach our eternal destination." [11]

This book discusses different doctrinal concepts that will help us rejoice as children of God and find more joy as we journey through life. If we don't follow Alma's counsel and test drive what is discussed, these chapters will merely be motivational pep talks, whose inspiration wears off after a short period of time. Only when we write spiritual knowledge on the "fleshy tables of the heart" (2 Corinthians 3:3) will we rise up as dedicated, vibrant, enthusiastic children of God who are thrilled to be who we are.

The end of each chapter includes a list of specific goals and steps that will help you apply what is discussed and develop faith and knowledge in the concepts in each chapter. If you take time to work on the suggestions, growing a little at a time, you can affect how you feel, think, and act. It is our thoughts, feelings, and actions that set us on the path to God and the pursuit of more peace and joy. This book is structured so that more fundamental ideas are first, followed by more involved concepts. However, you must work on the basics first, in order to have a strong foundation to build upon.

The time has come for us to grasp the concept of who we are and reach for the joy the Lord has waiting for us in this life. When the brother of Jared brought the sixteen small stones to the mountain, the Lord touched them and filled them with light (Ether 3:4–5). Likewise, if we bring our heart and soul to the Lord, he will touch them, filling them with happiness and joy. As we follow Christ and come to understand the great plan of happiness and our personal place in it, we will radiate that joy and knowledge for the world to see. Not only can we have joy when we return to our Heavenly Father, but we can rejoice along the way.

NOTES

1. Pew Research Center, "Are We Happy Yet?" online at http://pewresearch.org.
2. Claudia Wallis, "The New Science of Happiness," Feb. 21, 2005, *Time*, online at www.time.com.
3. Martin E. P. Seligman, *Authentic Happiness* (New York: Free Press, 2002), 8.
4. Ibid.
5. Ibid.
6. Ibid.
7. Dallin H. Oaks, "Preparation for the Second Coming," *Ensign*, May 2004, 7.
8. Richard D. Draper, *A Fulness of Joy* (American Fork, Utah: Covenant Communications, 2002), 18.
9. Marion G. Romney, "Satan—The Great Deceiver," *Ensign*, June 1971, 35.
10. Neal A. Maxwell, *That Ye May Believe* (Salt Lake City: Bookcraft, 1992), 101.
11. Robert D. Hales, "To Act for Ourselves: The Gift and Blessings of Agency," *Ensign*, May 2006, 4; emphasis added.

CHAPTER THREE

Resolve Your Identity Crisis

EVERYONE LOVES A SUPERHERO. Recently
there has been an upsurge of interest in characters and stories that were
once on the pages of comic books. At one time or other, many of these
superheroes go through an identity crisis. Spiderman, Batman, and
Superman, for instance, all have times when their secret identity makes
their everyday existence agonizing. For our entertainment, a variety of
scenarios and solutions play themselves out as the superheroes struggle to
decide which identity to embrace.

Although we are not superheroes that must maintain a secret identity,
we place great stock in our individuality. Teenagers in particular spend
enormous energy to discover and display their individuality. We jealously
guard our sense of self and work hard to define who we are.

In psychology, an identity crisis is actually an important developmen-
tal stage and is believed to be one of the most important conflicts human
beings encounter as they grow and develop. Erik Erikson, the psychologist who coined the phrase identity crisis, contended that only individuals
who succeed in resolving their crises and become comfortable with their
identities will be ready to face future challenges in life.

Every one of us faces a spiritual identity crisis while on earth. When
we are born and our memories of the premortal life are veiled, we must
rediscover who we are. Individually we must realize, define, and understand our true identity. Although in psychology the identity crisis stage
usually occurs in adolescence, we can spend years—even our entire
lives—struggling with a spiritual identity crisis. Only when we resolve

this crisis will we be ready to face future challenges, especially in these latter days. The first step in finding joy is coming to a true understanding of who we are.

KNOW WHO YOU ARE

Remember the prophecies about the condition of the days we live in? The Lord knows what things are like in the last days, and he knows how to help his children not only survive the ugliness and turmoil, but find joy and be valiant in such conditions. And it starts by resolving your identity crisis.

If Satan can disrupt our progress at this first crucial step, then it will take less work to prevent us from reaching our spiritual potential. All he has to do is make us forget who we really are. Unfortunately it doesn't seem to take a whole lot to make us forget, and Satan's playbook is varied and tested. He can distract us, urge us to be frantically busy, or entice us to focus on non-eternal things, to name just a few tactics. When we forget who we really are, we may forget why we are really here.

I had a pivotal experience that helped remember who I really am. My husband and I dated for a long time before I was even open to the idea of marriage. Without realizing it, I had fallen into some of the world's way of thinking. I had dreams to pursue, things to do, and great works to accomplish before I could settle down into the "boring" role of wife and mother.

At other times, I was nagged by the idea that somehow I was not good enough for the wonderful man who had proposed to me. I had no doubt that my husband was one of the noble and great ones spoken of by Abraham (Abraham 3:22), but I was convinced that I was not included in that description. Why should a noble and great man become shackled to mediocre and insignificant little me? My future husband did not know what was the matter with me, but when I shared what was wrong, he gave me a shoulder to cry on, looked deeply into my eyes, and told me that I was being foolish.

Fortunately, a blunt fiancé and a loving Father in Heaven helped me change some of my attitudes and gain a more eternal picture of God's plans for my happiness. It was still painful and hard. I felt like I would be giving up my only chance to accomplish some cherished desires. However, I also knew, through several real and vivid experiences, that the Good

Shepherd was lovingly encouraging me to take this vital step. Had I clung to the deceptive and debasing lies of Satan, things would have turned out differently for me.

It is imperative that you recognize your glorious potential. You are not here on this earth at this time merely to be a nameless audience member watching the "noble and great ones" do their marvelous works. *You are one of them!* The fact that you are who you are means that you belong to the noble and great community.

"That we are here now," Sheri L. Dew reminds us, "is no accident. For aeons of time our Father watched us and knew He could trust us when so much would be at stake. We have been held in reserve for this very hour. We need to understand not just who we are but who we have always been."[1]

YOU ARE A CHILD OF GOD

The world today is more informal than ever before. Paternity and bloodlines mean less than they did throughout much of history. Years ago, a person's ancestry and parentage were often of utmost importance, more so than a person's occupation, personality, or behavior. No matter what someone achieved, it was nearly impossible to break out of the social position to which a person was born. Conversely, no matter to what low the aristocracy might descend, persons of privilege often escaped justice and retribution because of their bloodline.

Centuries of revolution, revelation, and accessible education have eroded the entitlements and privileges once associated with ancestry, placing large groups of people throughout the world on more equal footing. On the other hand, as the influence of lineage has faded away, so too has the ennobling sense that we are the literal spiritual offspring of the King of Kings. Satan has worked hard to sever the familial spiritual bonds linking us to the Father and to each other, and has even convinced many that we are merely animals, the latest result of a random evolutionary cycle.

We affirm that we are each a child of God, but do we really consider what that means? Certain people, such as royalty, still possess a high regard for birthright. From childhood they know who they are and are schooled in their role and duties. Likewise, spiritually we are of noble birth—we are heavenly princes and princesses. Just as earthly royalty are taught their role and duties in academies and finishing schools, so too are we, as children of the Mighty God, being schooled and taught by our experiences here on earth to fulfill the divine heritage that is ours.

Brigham Young once said, "Instead of receiving the Gospel to *become* the sons [and daughters] of God, my language would be—to receive the Gospel that we may *continue* to be the sons [and daughters] of God."[2] We are heirs to the throne of our Heavenly Father just as Prince William is heir to the throne of England.

The fact that we are children of God is a fairly simple concept on the surface, yet it has deep significance. We may not completely understand all the ramifications of our spiritual bloodline until the next life, but there are some conclusions we can draw now. So, what does being a child of God mean?

WHAT DOES BEING A CHILD OF GOD MEAN?

We have to begin with our understanding of God, because, spiritually, it underlies everything. Many consider God an omnipotent presence, some sort of inconceivable and immaterial power just floating around. Another popular view of God is the idea of a "Watchmaker God," a deity that simply put the components together and then stepped back to let his creation tick away, thus ending his connection with us. Others eliminate God from the equation completely. All of these ideas depersonalize God and his involvement with us, making him distant and unapproachable.

Thankfully, the truth of God's nature has been restored and the Church's doctrine of God is very clear. First of all, being a child of God means that God is your father. Our spirits are literal sons and daughters of a very real Heavenly Father, who has genuine love and concern for us. In fact, our Father in Heaven is the very best father you can imagine. He is perfect! All the might, power, glory, and majesty in the universe is possessed by him. Better yet, all this glory and power is not held by a celebrity, an ivory tower intellectual, or some eccentric billionaire like we are accustomed to seeing here on earth. This awesome, glorious, omnipotent being is your dad!

Although we teach this concept to children when they can barely walk and talk, to some extent we sometimes treat our Heavenly Father like those who do not have the restored truth. Rather than seeing him as our dad, with whom we can have a personal relationship, we hesitate to approach him. Perhaps we feel like he is too busy to notice us, or maybe that he disapproves of how short we fall of perfection. Most often, I believe that to us he is simply a stranger, since for whatever reason we have not forged an intimate, personal relationship with him.

Think about those on Earth who are trying to be good parents. How many of them want the best for their child? How many rejoice when their child is happy? How many hate to see their child sad? How many work hard to help their child succeed? How many parents do all they can to meet their child's needs? These things are part of being a good parent. Why then do we often act like, or even believe, that our Heavenly Father is less concerned about our welfare than an earthly parent would be?

This is not a new attitude. In the New Testament, the Savior asked, "What man is there of you, whom if his son ask bread, will he give him a stone? Or if he ask a fish, will he give him a serpent?" (Matthew 7:9–10). What father is going to give his children useless or dangerous things while disregarding the true needs of his child? And, I would add, what good father would ignore his child's plea for necessities?

"If ye then, being evil [see footnote 11a: *although you are wicked*], know how to give good gifts unto your children, how much more shall your Father which is in heaven give good things to them that ask him?" (Matthew 7:11). So if we, who are imperfect and sin all the time, still know how to give good things to our children, then how much better is a perfect Father at giving his children what they need? (Note that it is what they *need*, not necessarily what they *want*.)

President Harold B. Lee said, "What a delightful reflection for his servants, to draw nigh to their Father, as to an endearing parent, and ask for blessings, as a son would ask for bread, and be confident of receiving. . . . And if the world could comprehend, how gladly would they throw themselves upon his guardianship, seek his wisdom and government, and claim a father's benediction; but Satan has blinded the eyes of the world, and they know not the things which make for their peace."[3]

Our earthly relationships provide a foundational understanding for our heavenly relationships. First of all, when we become parents ourselves, we obtain valuable insight and appreciation for our own Heavenly Father. Just as Abraham received a greater understanding through his trial with Isaac, so do our own parental ordeals enlarge our discernment in a way that cannot be duplicated by any other means.

For example, good parenting frequently involves telling a child no. Sometimes when the answer is yes, it is often followed by the stipulation "but not until later." And how often do we make our children earn something they want through good behavior or work? Yet when our Heavenly Father answers us in these ways, we ourselves sometimes act just like a whiny child!

Secondly, our relationship with our own earthly father often lays the groundwork for the important relationship with our Father in Heaven. I did not understand the importance an earthly father played in my attitude toward my Eternal Father until after I was married. My parents divorced when I was a toddler, and my mother raised three children on her own. We moved near her mother and sister—also divorcées—and so we became an extended family unit run primarily by women. My older brother was the only male around, and to be honest I didn't really miss having a dad. I didn't know any different. We were doing just fine without men (and we were also very politically correct in our feminine independence).

For me, not having a father-daughter relationship here on earth handicapped my own relationship with my Heavenly Father. Since I did not sense the importance of a close, personal relationship with my own father, I had trouble extending that bond to my Father in Heaven. My comprehension of this personal stumbling block has grown in large part through watching my husband and his father. I can see how the quality of that relationship carries over into my husband's spiritual connection with Heavenly Father. And I now realize even more the importance of my husband's relationship with our children and how that will in turn influence their feelings toward their Heavenly Father.

Satan has had thousands of years to fine-tune his methods, and he is most efficient if he can undermine our relationship with and confidence in our Eternal Father. One way to do this is to remove the influence of the father in the home. The number of out-of-wedlock births and single mother families is on the rise. As more adults divorce and remarry multiple times, or choose to simply live together until they become discontent and move on to the next partner, children often see fathers as men merely passing in and out of their lives. When a father is not a constant—or even important—presence, and the children must struggle to be close to a father they can see and touch, how much more difficult will it be for them to develop a healthy relationship with a father who is much less immediately perceivable?

This disturbing trend to devalue fatherhood obscures the truth that we can depend on our Father in Heaven even more than our earthly fathers. Our spirit is who we are even more so than our bodies. Therefore, the father of your spirit is more your father than your earthly father. As much as earthly fathers know their children, our spiritual father knows his children far more—even better than they know themselves.

The Lord knows each of us. He knows your name. He knows your favorite pastimes, what you like to eat, and those things that get under your skin. He revels in your strengths and has compassion for your weaknesses. The Lord knows your heart, including the dreams and fears you barely acknowledge to yourself. He knows your struggles, your triumphs, and all the times in between. The Lord knows you well, and to have real, lasting joy, you must strive to know him in return.

When we return to the heavenly home from which we came, I imagine that we will be astonished by numerous things. Of all the many wondrous and amazing things we will see and know, the prophet Ezra Taft Benson said, "Nothing is going to startle us more when we pass through the veil to the other side than to realize how well we know our Father and how familiar his face is to us."[4]

President Brigham Young stated that if we could see our Heavenly Father, we would realize that we do know him. He said, "I want to tell you, each and every one of you, that you are well acquainted with God our Heavenly Father. . . . You are all well acquainted with him, for there is not a soul of you but what has lived in his house and dwelt with him year after year; and yet you are seeking to become acquainted with him, when the fact is, you have merely forgotten what you did know."[5]

You are a child of God, and that means that you know your Eternal Father well, and he knows you even better. You just don't remember the tender bonds formed eons ago. That means that all of us must become reacquainted with God all over again while here on this earth. Our Father in Heaven has extended the invitation for each of us to personally know him, to feel for ourselves his love for us, and to have the joy that knowledge gives us.

THE DEPTH OF GOD'S LOVE

Being a child of God does not mean that we are just spirit children of God. He has told us that we are his *beloved* spirit sons and daughters. Synonyms for beloved are cherished, treasured, adored, preferred, precious, dear, favored, and wanted. To our Heavenly Father you are not "just his child," you are his beloved child—special, cherished, and precious. The incredible thing is that we all are beloved children of God. This does not in any way diminish our Eternal Father's feelings toward each child individually. As a perfect parent, he has more than enough love for all of us.

In this world we come in contact with many kinds of love. We see romantic love, lustful love, selfish love, the love of friendship, smothering or obsessive love, childish love, unrequited love, and needy love, just to name a few. God's love is more than any of these. Not only is his love validating, but it moves us forward toward him; it produces growth and change in us. Our Father's love not only improves us but also clarifies things. Elder John H. Groberg said, "When filled with God's love, we can do and see and understand things that we could not otherwise do or see or understand. Filled with His love, we can endure pain, quell fear, forgive freely, avoid contention, renew strength, and bless and help others in ways surprising even to us."[6]

When others speak of my family friends the Bishops, invariably they express the sentiment that the Bishops truly love other people. At one point I wondered if it was this love for others that brought them so much joy. They told me that their deep, outward-reaching love for others only came after they felt the Lord's love for them personally. They treat others the way they do because they know how much God loves them and, therefore, how much he loves his other children. The Bishops know they are beloved children of God, and they view others that way. This knowledge brings them joy, and joy to others as well.

Our Father in Heaven loves all of his children all of the time. Our ability to feel his love, however, comes and goes. I am incredibly blessed, yet I struggle to feel his love for me every day. We should strive to feel this closeness regularly, because partaking in God's love for you individually is a big step toward finding joy in life's journey. The steps at the end of this chapter can help you do this. Our pursuit of joy hastens as we gain an appreciation for the depth of our Father's love and his desire to be near us and to help and heal us.

Although it may be hard in mortality for us to grasp the depth of our Heavenly Father's love for his children, we catch a glimpse in the Pearl of Great Price. The Lord showed the prophet Enoch all of his creations, and Enoch not only saw the glory and majesty of God, but also the great hold Satan had upon the hearts of all the nations. To Enoch's astonishment, the Lord then wept.

Enoch was amazed. He had just seen the multitude and glory of God's creations and knew that the Lord had just taken up Zion to dwell with him in peace forever. With all these wonderful things, how can the great Creator weep?

We can feel the heartache of a tender and loving parent in the Lord's reply. The Father lamented what his beautiful children were doing to each other and to themselves with the knowledge and agency he gave them. God explained the unalterable truth that his wicked children must be punished to satisfy justice. A loving Father was weeping for the choices made by his children and the resulting consequences of those choices (Moses 7:23–40).

In seeing the depth of God's love, Enoch then "knew, and looked upon their wickedness, and their misery, and wept and stretched forth his arms, and his heart swelled wide as eternity; and his bowels yearned; and all eternity shook" (Moses 7:41). Enoch was able to see his brothers and sisters through the eyes of a loving heavenly parent.

While Enoch was fortunate enough to momentarily glimpse the Creation, man, and the eternities through the Father's eyes, for most of us "it doth not yet appear what we shall be" (1 John 3:2). The natural man clouds our vision and obscures our view. In this mortal sphere we get to know the natural man (or woman) so well that we often become completely blind to who we were before the natural man became a part of us. And genuine self-worth is found through our internal, and eternal, selves, not the natural man we too often focus on.

When we concentrate too much on the external natural man, we far too often consider ourselves as insignificant or unimportant. We all go through times when—for whatever reason—we feel of little worth, but in reality our worth is inestimable. The Lord himself told us "the worth of souls is great in the sight of God" (D&C 18:10). Elder Marvin J. Ashton said, "I am certain our Heavenly Father is displeased when we refer to ourselves as 'nobody.' . . . We do ourselves a great injustice when we allow ourselves . . . to so identify ourselves. No matter how or where we find ourselves, we cannot with any justification, label ourselves 'nobody.' As children of God we are somebody."[7]

We are each the beloved son or daughter of a God, and since we can't remember or fully grasp the magnitude of Godhood, we actually have no idea what our potential really is. All we really know is that we are in the process of becoming who we are. When we come to know God, we can come to truly know ourselves and our eternal, infinite worth.

FROM IDENTITY TO ACTION

This mortal life has an abundance of opportunities to use the agency God has given us. Elder Robert D. Hales tells those who have become ensnared by dangerous behaviors that the first thing they can do to climb out of their spiritual black hole is to "*choose* to accept—truly accept—that [they] are a child of God, that He loves [them], and that He has the power to help [them]."[8] If a sense of our true identity is powerful enough to help those addicted to destructive influences, then certainly it can help those who are merely spiritually stagnant, as well as anything in between.

Many of God's servants have told us that knowledge of our eternal identity is of utmost importance. Elder Dallin H. Oaks called it "a potent antidepressant" that "can strengthen each of us to make righteous choices and to seek the best that is within us."[9]

Just like the angle at which an arrow is fired determines the distance it will travel, our basic assumptions about ourselves determine the paths we will choose. Joan B. McDonald, author of *The Holiness of Everyday Life*, urges us to change these assumptions. She writes, "We were first children of God. And we are becoming that which we already are—Gods to be. When we act from that assumption, we can focus on the light and goodness within ourselves and the light that leads us on. We become more conscious of, and more responsive to, our yearnings to be close to and act like God. Gradually, throughout eternity, the natural man falls away, and, like a snake shedding its skin, our truer selves come to light and move toward God."[10]

We are not surprised when a child exhibits similar traits as her parents. If a mother and father are really tall, you anticipate that their children will also be tall. Athletic parents often have athletic children, very intelligent parents frequently have very intelligent children, and so on. "It's in his blood" and "It's in her genes" are common expressions. Many times, children grow up to be like their parents in many respects.

Likewise, each child of Heavenly Father inherited capacities and characteristics from her divine parents. All spirit children of God inherited the potential needed to become like their Heavenly Father or Mother, else God's eternal plan would not work. To resolve our spiritual identity crisis we must internalize the idea that being a child of God means that in truth we can "grow up" to be like our heavenly parents and that we have more potential than we can imagine.

Even though we have inherited divine potential by virtue of our spiritual lineage, our capacities must still be faithfully developed. In mortality, if a person born with natural gifts and abilities does not develop them, then that person will never rise to his or her potential. We are truly "gods in embryo," but the development of our embryo is dependent upon our effort and spiritual growth.

Once you have confidence in your true identity, it will naturally influence your actions and your focus in life. A conviction that you are a son or daughter of God gives you a feeling of comfort in your self-worth. You do not need to spend time, energy, and money attempting to build your self-esteem through the fleeting trends of the day because you know where your true value lies: you are a child of the living God, and he loves you.

Identity is important. Someone once said, "It is not what people call you that matters; it is what you answer to that counts." No matter what others say about you, or what you think they say, or even what you may think about yourself, God has shared through his prophets who you really are. Then when tough times come, you can be secure in your worth and have that knowledge that will not only keep you afloat but allow you to withstand the temptations of the devil.

The Pearl of Great Price also shows how Moses overcame a personal attack from Satan by remembering his eternal identity. In the first chapter of Moses, God himself made sure that Moses understood that he was a child of God. The Lord then showed Moses a glorious vision of the world and its inhabitants, but this remarkable experience left Moses exhausted. At that time of weakness, Satan showed up to tempt him, saying, "Moses, *son of man*, worship me" (Moses 1:12; emphasis added).

Satan tried to attack Moses' understanding of who he was, but Moses responded with conviction. "And it came to pass that Moses looked upon Satan and said: Who art thou? For behold, *I am a son of God*, in the similitude of his Only Begotten; and where is thy glory, that I should worship thee?" (Moses 1:13; emphasis added).

Our prophet, Gordon B. Hinckley, exhorts us to come to a greater understanding of who we really are. He said, "There is a mighty strength that comes of the knowledge that you and I are sons and daughters of God. Within us is something of divinity. One who has this knowledge and permits it to influence his life will not stoop to do a mean or cheap or tawdry thing."[11] Perhaps if we truly understood who we are, we would be less likely to make choices that would lead us off the path of joy.

You are a child of God. As Latter-day Saints we hear it, we sing it, and we preach it. But do you truly believe it? The world would have you think that you find joy and happiness through self-esteem or self-confidence, but joy is found through a confident knowledge that God knows you, loves you, and stands ready to help you become what he knows you can become. Do you know who you are—really?

There comes a time when you just need to know, for yourself, the truth that you are a beloved son or daughter of God. Your loving Father in Heaven eagerly waits to reveal the depth of his love for you, but first you have to accept and believe. Then you must obtain a witness to the truth through the Spirit.

Knowledge received from the Spirit is revelation, and some knowledge can only be received in this way, simply because there is no other way to learn it. As Paul told us, "But the natural man receiveth not the things of the Spirit of God: for they are foolishness unto him: neither can he know them, because they are spiritually discerned" (1 Corinthians 2:14). Because of the veil placed over our memory, the only way that we can gain a firm, unshakable conviction that we are precious and beloved children of God is to turn to heaven and pray for it to be revealed to us. Just as Moroni counseled us to discover the truth of the Book of Mormon through prayer (Moroni 10:3–5), the doctrine of our divinity must one day penetrate our hearts through prayer as well.

Perhaps you have never thought to pray for this specific confirmation or maybe you just need to be reminded, but I urge you to make this a vital part of your daily prayers. Ask God if he loves you and if you really are his child. I promise you, your loving Father in Heaven will happily respond, and you will have joy when he does.

I am deeply thankful for the knowledge of who I am. I may not be famous or glamorous or possess widely acclaimed skill or talent. I am just a normal, often frazzled, stay-at-home mom, but I am a normal, often frazzled, stay-at-home mom who is the daughter of a Heavenly Father who dearly loves me. And when it comes down to it, that knowledge is worth more than worldly fame, beauty, or talent. Just as Nephi was grateful for the unseen hand of the Lord as it guided him safely through the streets of Jerusalem in his quest for the brass plates, I rejoice in the knowledge that I am a beloved daughter of God whose steps are guided, whose paths are made straight, and whose royal destiny lies in my Eternal Father's capable hands.

CHAPTER THREE STEPS

1. Set aside time to contemplate the truth of your divine parentage. Really think about and ponder it.
2. Pray for confirmation of the Lord's love for you personally. Do it often.
3. Write down a description of what you would consider a perfect father—what you would want in a father. Look at your list and visualize that Heavenly Father is all of those things and more.
4. Read the scriptures looking specifically for examples and clues to the nature of your Heavenly Father. This will help you get to know him and draw closer to him. Keep a list. For example: He always keeps his promises—2 Nephi 10:17. You may also want to include the characteristics of God from Joseph Smith's *Lectures on Faith* (lecture 3, sections 12–18).
5. Examine your list and ponder the idea that you have divine potential to grow in those qualities and characteristics to become more like your Father in Heaven.
6. Pick a quality from your list and focus for a month on refining that quality yourself. Understand that after a month you will not be perfect in that characteristic, but over time you will progress and improve.
7. Look for and record instances in your own life where you can see the hand of the Lord and his personal interest in you. Then when you have those times you doubt your own worth or the Lord's love for you, reread what you have written.
8. Also record experiences when the Lord didn't give you what you *wanted*, but in retrospect you realize that he gave you what you *needed*. Refer back to this at those times when you really want something but it seems the Lord isn't listening.
9. Do family history research and work. As you learn about your earthly forefathers, your relationship with your Heavenly Father will be enriched. The scripture, "And he shall turn the heart of the fathers to the children, and the heart of the children to their fathers" (Malachi 4:6) is not just referring to children and fathers in the mortal sense.
10. Think of others as your brothers and sisters. Honor the deity within others and your divine connection to them by treating them as children of God, just like you.

NOTES

1. Sheri L. Dew, "Stand Tall and Stand Together," 94.

2. John A. Widtsoe, comp., *Discourses of Brigham Young* (Salt Lake City: Deseret Book, 1978), 7; emphasis added.

3. John Taylor, *The Government of God* (Salt Lake City: 1852), 31.

4. Cited in Henry B. Eyring, "To Draw Closer to God," *Ensign*, May 1991, 65.

5. Widtsoe, *Discourses of Brigham Young*, 50.

6. John H. Groberg, "The Power of God's Love," *Ensign*, Nov. 2004, 11.

7. Marvin J. Ashton, "In His Strength," *Ensign*, July 1973, 24.

8. Robert D. Hales, "To Act for Ourselves: The Gift and Blessings of Agency," *Ensign*, May 2006, 4; emphasis added.

9. Dallin H. Oaks, "Powerful Ideas," *Ensign*, Nov. 1995, 25.

10. Joan B. MacDonald, *The Holiness of Everyday Life* (Salt Lake City: Deseret Book, 1995), 37–38.

11. Gordon B. Hinckley, "God Hath Not Given Us the Spirit of Fear," *Ensign*, Oct. 1984, 2.

CHAPTER FOUR

Fulfill the Measure of Your Creation

THE SEARCH FOR JOY

The first step in finding joy as you go through life is internalizing the glorious truth that you are a beloved son or daughter of God. Just as cygnets become swans, each of us has the potential to become like our heavenly parents—in fact, it is our destiny to do so. This not only entails being resurrected into a cleansed and spotless state as they are, it also means thinking, living, and basically becoming in every sense as they are. Since one of our Heavenly Father's distinguishing characteristics is that he is full of happiness and joy, it is not surprising that "happiness is the object and design of our existence; and will be the end thereof, if we pursue the path that leads to it."[1]

As mentioned previously, society is always looking for ways to be happier. On television, for example, we see a dizzying array of shows on ways that people can improve their living experience and pursue happiness and self-fulfillment. Travel shows, craft shows, home decorating shows, health shows, and home improvement shows all tout the idea that by following their advice your life will be fuller. You can also give your happiness a boost by having the perfect wedding, participating in outdoor adventures, learning how to play and win poker, learning how to live like celebrities, or mastering the way to live the life of luxury. All these shows are aimed at making your life better in some way—making it more beautiful, more impressive, or more perfect. Somehow, many have fallen for the notion that bigger, better, and more expensive will make us happier.

As people pursue happiness in these ways, they often become caught in a vicious cycle going from one thing to the next, searching for something that produces more than temporary good feelings. We have become a society of adults that act like children who desperately want a new toy, yet once they gets it all they can think about is a different toy that they now desperately want. We move from thing to thing to thing and are never satisfied. Unfortunately for those chasing happiness in this manner, worldly pleasures will always diminish and disappear eventually, leaving the seeker dissatisfied and empty. What everyone really wants is happiness that will last. They want joy.

Joy is more than happiness, and joy cannot be found where the world usually looks for it. Our yearnings for joy and happiness were implanted in our hearts by Deity, like a kind of homesickness, for we have a residual memory of our premortal existence. They are also a taste of what is promised to the faithful. The Book of Mormon makes it clear that happiness is our destiny and that we can dwell "with God in a state of never-ending happiness" (Mosiah 2:41).

All people are looking for happiness and joy, yet many good people who understand where joy lies, and try hard to find it there, have a hard time grasping it. At some time or another we all become weighed down with the serious tasks of daily living. Bills must be paid, children must be taught and cared for, and we must strive to live righteously. Some may even feel that church responsibilities merely add to the weight. Unfortunately, at these times we tend to let joy and excitement go out of our lives.

It's true that we can't help but worry sometimes, and there will always be problems and demands to deal with. However, don't let these natural challenges in life frustrate, discourage, and depress you to the point that your mind and attitude are distracted from the very principles that would help you rise above the negative and find the positive answers you need.

We are not on Earth to simply earn a living, relentlessly toil to fulfill all the responsibilities that weigh on our shoulders, and then finally have some joy after mortality is over. Imagine what life must have been like for Lehi's family as they traveled to the promised land. Living in the wilderness for years meant the days were filled with the mundane concerns of simple survival. Without a doubt, there were probably days, weeks, or even months where the group felt like they lived in a never-ending round of drudgery. And yet, in the midst of this travail came the resplendent vision of the tree of life, which is still applicable to us today in our modern never-ending round of drudgery.

The beautiful tree in Lehi's vision contained the key to obtaining "exceedingly great joy" (1 Nephi 8:12). When Nephi asked for the interpretation of his father's dream, he was told that the tree represented "the love of God" (1 Nephi 11:22). It was described as "most desirable above all things" and "the most joyous to the soul" (1 Nephi 11:22–23).

Lehi saw "numberless concourses of people, many of whom were pressing forward, that they might obtain the path which led unto the tree" (1 Nephi 8:21). Some attained their goal and actually commenced "in the path" (1 Nephi 8:22). However, most of the people in the vision did not even try; they did not know the correct path to joy. And among those who did walk the path, many were not able to stay the course.

Along the path that led to the tree, Lehi saw that "there arose a mist of darkness; yea, even an exceedingly great mist of darkness, insomuch that they who had commenced in the path did lose their way, that they wandered off and were lost" (1 Nephi 8:23). The devil's mist confused, distracted, or scared the travelers and obscured the path so that they lost their way. Those of us who have been baptized are already on the path toward the tree. We are already heading the right way to joy. The key to staying on the path lies in ignoring the mists of the devil.

Lehi was shown that there was only one way to successfully make it through the mists to the tree. "I beheld a rod of iron, and it extended along the bank of the river, and led to the tree by which I stood" (1 Nephi 8:19). He saw many "pressing forward . . . and they did press forward through the mist of darkness, clinging to the rod of iron, even until they did come forth and partake of the fruit of the tree" (1 Nephi 8:24). Nephi clarified that the rod of iron "was the word of God" (1 Nephi 11:25).

I once heard a talk by professor and author Randy Bott in which he discussed gyroscopic dissonance.[2] If nothing else, using that term got the audience's attention! A gyroscope is a spinning wheel on an axle used for measuring or maintaining orientation. Once spinning, a gyroscope will resist changes to its direction or course.

Through the Lord's plan, we are set on a course intended to lead us back to him. That we are here on this Earth proves that we were already on that path before our mortal birth. We were born with our orientation already pointed heavenward, and, like a gyroscope, our spirit, aided by the Light of Christ, will resist changes to this orientation. Because of this, we experience stress, anxiety, and resistance when we try to veer from our heavenward orientation. This is called dissonance—when one's professed belief system is being compromised by one's actions.

Each of us experience spiritual gyroscopic dissonance to some degree because we are still working toward perfection, and many times our actions will not be in accord with what we should do. At those times, this dissonance helps us repent and get oriented in the right direction again. Just as the Liahona guided Lehi's family to the promised land, when we have our personal gyroscopes lined up with the Lord—when we hold fast to the rod of iron—we can reach the tree of Lehi's vision and find joy, both in this life and in the hereafter.

It is important to note, however, that simply arriving at the tree does not assure us of eternal life, love, and happiness. Lehi watched many who tasted of the fruit and then were ashamed afterwards, "and they fell away into forbidden paths and were lost" (1 Nephi 8:28). They had finally reached their goal. They had even partaken of the fruit. They tasted and experienced that which was "the most joyous to the soul" (1 Nephi 11:23). Yet they still left. Why?

Many looked across the river of water and saw an impressive building. This great and spacious building beckoned alluringly, and numerous people left the tree to join those inside. Sadly, many others who had already partaken of God's love did not actually cross to the spacious building, but they could not ignore the mocking scorn of the world. When confronted by the pointing fingers and jeers of those in the building, these people were ashamed and fell away.

The fact that activities always forbidden by the Lord are now accepted and promoted by society make it increasingly difficult to firmly grasp the iron rod. Just compare what is talked about, shown, and even glorified now on a normal basis with what would have been allowed even as recent as a decade ago. Practices that would have been hidden as shameful are now flaunted and applauded. The media serves up these activities in a way that makes them look very desirable. Not only are they presented as appealing, but they are also shown as the way to be happy. We are relentlessly bombarded every day with the world's path to happiness.

As Lehi shared in his vision, the great and spacious building of the world is extremely enticing, especially when the people in the building seem to be having a great time. It is hard not to be drawn to where others seem so obviously happy. But all the world has to offer is instant, short-term gratification that is irrevocably connected to long-term sorrow and suffering. Elder Glen L. Pace warns us not to mistake telestial pleasure for celestial happiness and joy. "Don't mistake lack of self-control for freedom. Complete freedom without appropriate restraint makes us slaves to our appetites. Don't envy a lesser and lower life."[3]

Those who yield to the enticing of Satan may, as the scripture says, "enjoy the pleasures of sin for a season" (Hebrews 11:25), but that kind of pleasure can never lead to lasting happiness or eternal joy. The seasons always, always change. Those who pursue Satan's way are certain to have Satan's misery. Unless they repent, they will "remain with the father of lies, in misery, like unto himself" (2 Nephi 9:9). As Alma told his wayward son, "wickedness never was happiness" (Alma 41:10).

Lehi also gave us the key to avoiding the great-and-spacious-building pitfall. Nephi said, those in the great building "did point the finger of scorn at me and those that were partaking of the fruit also; but we heeded them not" (1 Nephi 8:33). The faithful gave no heed; they ignored the rejection, scorn, and ridicule of the world. They did not pay attention to the great and spacious building or its occupants. Not only did they not fear the world, but they also had no interest in what the world offered. Once we reach the tree and partake of the fruit of life, we must be willing to ignore the world.

Is ignoring the world difficult to do? Sometimes, but it can be done. I am not a big shopper. My husband jokingly calls me the penny Nazi, but I like to consider myself frugal. One of my tactics to avoid unnecessary purchases is to simply not go to the store. This approach also works when I try to ignore the world. I merely do not let some things in my house or life at all.

A song from my high school years gave the advice, "Don't read beauty magazines; they will only make you feel ugly." Similarly, don't pay attention to those things that glamorize lifestyles in conflict with the Lord's commandments. They will only make you feel as if you are missing out. If you don't even flirt with the world, it will be much easier to ignore it.

Another thing we do to help our children ignore the world is offer good alternatives to worldly clamor. For example, we restrict the amount of time our children are exposed to violence or other questionable things on TV or video games. We encourage them to play at home and bring their friends, and so we have a cupboard stocked with games, a basement dedicated for large forts or club meetings, and a yard complete with basketball hoop, soccer goals, and lots of room to run around. As our children get older, we will adjust our fun things to match their ages so they will still want to be home. The same idea can work for us spiritually. If we fill our lives with good things, the world has less room to maneuver and get our attention.

I want to note that filling our lives with good things does not necessarily mean "churchy" things. You need not dedicate every spare minute to reading scriptures or listening to hymns (although that wouldn't necessarily be a bad choice). There are many good books, uplifting choices in music, and soul-expanding pastimes. Spending quality time with family and friends is one of the best things you can do with your time. Search out those things that elevate, develop character, and draw you closer to the refinement of heaven. You will have more joy as you fill your life with good things.

The Lord has provided us with the way to get through Satan's mists of darkness to the tree of life and then stay there, partaking of the fruit that is the most desirable and joyous to the soul. Despite what many believe, the way to happiness is not a complex puzzle that requires deep philosophical thought to discover. The best way is not necessarily the hardest way. President Benson told us in plain and simple language, "The gospel plan is the plan by which men are brought to a fulness of joy. . . . The gospel principles are the steps and guidelines that will help us find true happiness and joy."[4]

THAT WE MIGHT HAVE JOY

Many years after Lehi's marvelous vision, as he lay on his deathbed, Lehi left his children with the words he felt were the most important for them to remember. He said this seemingly simple statement, "Adam fell that men might be; and men are, that they might have joy" (2 Nephi 2:25). This thought is so succinct that it is easy to dismiss or pass over it without realizing its full significance.

We are not here merely to be happy, but to find our way to receive a fulness of joy (Psalm 16:11). To fulfill the measure of our creation is to have the joy our Eternal Father plans for us. Joy is deeper and longer lasting than happiness. Happiness relies heavily on the present; joy is much more long term. Joy often comes from anticipating a future reward that grows out of the necessary trials of the present. We must understand that sometimes we have to forsake momentary happiness so we can experience lasting joy in the future. It is very possible to go through periods of unhappiness and still possess joy.

I refer back now to Positive Psychologists who have also looked into the concept that people can be happy in the midst of bad events. They asked: In order to feel more happiness, should we try to experience less negative emotion by minimizing bad events in our lives? The answer was surprising. Contrary to popular belief, having more than your share of misery does not mean you cannot have a lot of joy as well.[5] A series of bad events does not doom you to a joyless existence.

The Prophet Joseph Smith was well acquainted with grief and sorrow. Not only did he have to personally endure trials, arrests, ridicule, attacks, imprisonments, threats, and being driven out of town, but six of his thirteen children also died in infancy or when very young. Despite all these horrible events, Joseph Smith was one of the most joyful men. Others actually criticized him at times for his native cheerfulness.[6] As Joseph Smith showed us, we can feel joy and be happy even with sorrow and despair.

In fact, sorrow and misery are necessary to truly appreciate joy. Father Lehi explained that if Adam and Eve had not gone through the process we call the Fall, they would have remained forever in their initial state of innocence, "having no joy, for they knew no misery; doing no good, for they knew no sin" (2 Nephi 2:23). Without misery, Adam and Eve could not have felt joy.

Even though we look forward to a fulness of joy after the Resurrection, that does not exclude joy in this life as well. President Ezra Taft Benson taught, "Everyone will have problems, disappointments, heartaches. It isn't on the pinnacle of success and ease where men and women grow into strong characters. But God intended that this life be essentially a satisfying and joyous life."[7] True joy can be experienced in this life *and* in the life to come.

Our first parents understood this. Adam blessed the name of the Lord, declaring, "Because of my transgression my eyes are opened, and *in this life I shall have joy*" (Moses 5:10; emphasis added). We should remember that even though we strive for the inexpressible joy of eternal life in the future, we can also feel joy in the present. Our Heavenly Father intends that we find joy in the journey.

LIVE WELL

Elder Sterling W. Sill expressed the idea that life has three dimensions:

> First, there is the length of life—or how long we live. Second, there is the breadth of life—or how interestingly we live. Third, there is the depth of life—or how much we live, represented by those great qualities of love, worship, devotion, service, etc. . . . The objective of life is not only to live long, but also to live well. . . . And when we have finally proved ourselves worthy of exaltation, then eternity will be the measure of life's length; celestial glory will be the measure of its breadth; to be like God will be the measure of its depth.[8]

How many times in church do we hear a comment or story prefaced with the words, "When I was on my mission . . ."? We may roll our eyes, but it is interesting to note how eighteen to twenty-four months can make such a big impact on people. A mission is just a short period of time, full of hard work and rejection, and with very little time to pursue fun. Yet many returned missionaries insist that the time on their mission was the best of their life. Using Elder Sill's dimensions, a missionary's life is so great because it is full of love, worship, devotion, and service. Those who got the most from their missions didn't just live, but lived well (according to the Lord's guidelines), and as a result they loved it.

We are not to just live life, but to live it well and love it. Nothing helps us accomplish this more than the correct attitude. Sister Elaine L. Jack, former general Relief Society president, counsels us to "get a life." She says, "We are sons and daughters of God. We have the fulness of the gospel of Jesus Christ. We are called to rise, not wallow. Brothers and sisters, let's get a life."[9]

A great example of the power of attitude is found in the juxtaposition of Nephi with his older brothers Laman and Lemuel. Even though you probably know it well, it's a great lesson worth repeating. As they traveled through the wilderness, Nephi experienced the same hardships as Laman and Lemuel (even more so because they were never tied up or beaten by *their* brothers), and yet listen to the two different descriptions of the same events. Nephi said:

> And so great were the blessings of the Lord upon us, that while we did live upon raw meat in the wilderness, our women did give plenty of suck for their children, and were strong, yea, even like unto the men; and they began to bear their journeyings without murmurings.

And thus we see that the commandments of God must be fulfilled. And if it so be that the children of men keep the commandments of God he doth nourish them, and strengthen them, and provide means whereby they can accomplish the thing which he has commanded them; wherefore, he did provide means for us while we did sojourn in the wilderness. (1 Nephi 17:2–3)

Contrast that with his brothers' viewpoint:

We have wandered in the wilderness for these many years; and our women have toiled, being big with child; and they have borne children in the wilderness and suffered all things, save it were death; and it would have been better that they had died before they came out of Jerusalem than to have suffered these afflictions.

Behold, these many years we have suffered in the wilderness, which time we might have enjoyed our possessions and the land of our inheritance; yea, and we might have been happy. (1 Nephi 17:20–21)

As humans we often tend to emphasize the negative, even when there is so much to be positive about. These days society as a whole tends to be pessimistic and skeptical. There is too much whining about a good thing ending and too little celebrating that it even happened in the first place. Newspapers and television reports center attention on tragedy, misery, and destruction. It can be hard to rise above the pervasive feeling of gloom surrounding us because we live in an age when, as the Lord foretold, men's hearts are failing them, not only physically but in spirit (D&C 45:26). If we are always focusing on the negative, how can we have room in our thoughts and hearts for joy?

A negative outlook on life not only robs us of potential happiness, but "dwelling on negative thoughts and approaches is, in fact, working directly opposite of hope, faith, and trust—in the Lord, ourselves, and others."[10] In contrast, the positive lifts and buoys us up and encourages us to forge ahead. Think about it. Would you rather be around a pessimist or an optimist?

I have a good friend whose seven-year-old son was diagnosed with brain cancer. Throughout his intensive chemotherapy and radiation treatment, he had a profound impact on many people through his amazing attitude. His positive outlook has inspired his family, our ward, the doctors and nurses, and even strangers at stores and other public places. You wouldn't think that a seven-year-old would be joyful in the middle of demanding treatment, but this little boy was. Testimonies have been strengthened and lives have been uplifted by his optimism in the face of such formidable challenges.

Many years ago, President Joseph F. Smith wisely counseled, "It is a matter of the greatest importance that the people be educated to appreciate and cultivate the bright side of life rather than to permit its darkness and shadows to hover over them."[11] We are told to "be of good cheer" (John 16:33), and Elder Neal A. Maxwell informed us that "in these days, being of good cheer is part of being valiant in the testimony of Jesus."[12]

Ezra Taft Benson said:

> As the showdown between good and evil approaches, with its accompanying trials and tribulations, Satan is increasingly striving to overcome the Saints with despair, discouragement, despondency, and depression.
>
> Yet, of all people, we as Latter-day Saints should be the most optimistic and the least pessimistic. For while we know that "peace shall be taken from the earth, and the devil shall have power over his own dominion," we are also assured that "the Lord shall have power over his saints, and shall reign in their midst" (D&C 1:35–36).[13]

Prior to the emergence of modern psychology, the Lord's servants knew the importance of a positive attitude. Proverbs states, "For as he thinketh in his heart, so is he" (Proverbs 23:7). Basically, what you focus on, you get.

Positive psychology has also found numerous benefits of a positive outlook on life. "Optimism and hope cause better resistance to depression when bad events strike, better performance at work, particularly in challenging jobs, and better physical health."[14] We need to develop a cheerful disposition not only for these benefits, but because gloom and pessimism make it harder for the Spirit to dwell with us and for faith to have place in our hearts.

My mother and grandmother participated in one of the first handcart treks put on by the Church years ago. They say that it was unbelievably hard, more like Zion's Camp than just a handcart trek. They walked fifty miles in the heat of midsummer, through the nights, with scarce water and very little food. Lowry Bishop, the same Brother Bishop I mentioned before, was assigned as the priesthood leader for their little "family," and his positive attitude was astonishing to behold. He was always upbeat, and his voice could be heard up and down the train of travelers, cheering them on, motivating and encouraging them, and singing songs. The amazing thing was that the entire time, Brother Bishop was in terrible pain from a bad stomach ulcer, which was exacerbated by insufficient food and water. Yet he never once complained. His example is still remembered by many who made that trek, and I know they draw on the memory to help them in their own trials.

We can be negative and look for the ugly in life, or we can be positive and see the beautiful around us. We can choose to focus on the faults and failings of others, or we can develop positive attitudes and see the good, the strong, the decent, and the virtuous in people. It is a matter of attitude. Would we rather emulate Nephi, or Laman and Lemuel?

ENJOY DAILY LIVING

Almost every technological advance in recent times has been about doing more and doing it faster. Today we also place a high value on planning for the future. As we do things faster while constantly focusing on the future, we can lose out on the present. Often we act and interact automatically, without much thinking. As such, we fail to notice huge chunks of experience. We neglect to savor, as Elaine L. Jack calls it, "the dailiness of living."[15]

Do you ever find yourself wishing present experiences could soon be over, because you think you might be happier doing something else? As a mother of young children, I sometimes find myself counting down the minutes until the children go to school, take a nap, or go to bed. At these times I fail to enjoy the moments I have with them because I am too busy marking time until they are out of my way. When I am in this mind-set, I forget that it is not the grand events that make up life, but all the little moments that together add up to living.

After surviving multiple brain surgeries, my friend's son was given very little time to recuperate because they had to begin treatment as soon as possible. The doctors impressed upon his mother how crucial it would be to focus on enjoying daily living with her child. They told her again and again to celebrate the little victories and cheer every happy event in her son's life during treatment. She took this advice to heart. We had a "Bald-Day Party" when his hair fell out, we threw mini celebrations when he made it through a round of chemotherapy, family arranged for him to ride in a parade, he participated in a huge fund-raising yard sale, neighbors brought over their children to play when he felt up to it or just to visit when he didn't, people brought over teddy bears or toys, and so forth.

As the months stacked up and the going got even harder, my friend continued to focus on celebrating life. After a year of exhausting treatment, my friend testifies to the importance of enjoying daily living. Not only was she unsure how many days her son would have left to enjoy, but she could also see the physical difference his happiness made. The doctors were right in saying her son's attitude and the attitudes of those around him were just as important as what the doctors did.

Do you take time to discover each day how beautiful your life can be? It can be hard to do this if we have packed too much in our lives. I sometimes catch myself becoming discouraged as I try to do it all. At those times, though I am frantically busy accomplishing things, I often manage to become irritated that I can't do more. Then entire days go by and I realize I have not taken any time to enjoy living, because I was too busy fretting over my impossible to-do list. No one can be Superman, and we will only burn ourselves out if we obsess over it.

We need to slow down and try to live in the now more often. This somehow seems easier to do when we escape into nature. Have you ever noticed how you feel when you enjoy the beauty of mountains, lakes, or oceans? While camping, hiking, or just visiting natural parks, it's somehow easier to consciously stop and drink in nature's beauty. To rejoice in the day-to-day moments of life we need to pause more frequently and notice the little things. (Ironically, I found my ability to do this rapidly decreasing as the publishing deadline for this book approached.) Enjoy your child's laughter, the feel of a soft blanket, or the warmth of the sun on your face.

One way to cultivate enjoyment of daily life is to be more grateful for what you have. University of California at Riverside psychologist Sonja Lyubomirsky discovered that promoting a feeling of gratitude was one of the best ways to lift someone's level of happiness. Some of her research subjects took time to conscientiously count their blessings once a week, and they significantly increased their overall satisfaction with life over a control group that did not count blessings.[16]

Other psychologists have found that gratitude can do more than lift one's mood. At the University of California at Davis, psychologist Robert Emmons found that gratitude exercises also "improve physical health, raise energy levels and, for patients with neuromuscular disease, relieve pain and fatigue."[17] There is a lot of power in a little appreciation!

These findings should not surprise members of the LDS Church. Our current prophet has often emphasized the importance of gratitude. In his book *Way to Be!*, President Hinckley lists being grateful as the first attribute in making life better, fuller, and more satisfying. He says, "Gratitude creates the most wonderful feeling. It can resolve disputes. It can strengthen friendships. And it makes us better men and women."[18]

It is easy to fall into the habit of ingratitude, especially when much of the world is on the acquisition treadmill, never satisfied by what they already have and always wanting more. There is a great tendency for us to always look for additional blessings, yet most of us probably don't think of ingratitude as a serious sin. However, the Prophet Joseph Smith said that one of the worst sins the Latter-day Saints would be guilty of would be the sin of ingratitude.[19]

The Lord himself has told us his view: "And in nothing doth man offend God, or against none is his wrath kindled, save those who confess not his hand in all things" (D&C 59:21). Those who confess not his hand in all things are those who are not grateful for what he has given.

To his grateful followers, though, the Lord has said, "And he who receiveth all things with thankfulness shall be made glorious; and the things of this earth shall be added unto him, even an hundred fold, yea, more" (D&C 78:19). The great principle of gratitude, when incorporated into our daily lives and prayers, can lift and bless us individually and collectively. When we take time to notice our blessings and enjoy daily living, we will discover more joy as we live it.

A FULNESS OF JOY

Men are that they might have joy, and we can do much to improve our happiness. Always remember, however, that the fulness of joy spoken of in the scriptures cannot be achieved through our own efforts, or even in this world (D&C 101:36). Only in Christ can our joy be completely full.

We can only have a fulness of joy when spirit and body are inseparably connected in the glorious resurrection to celestial glory (D&C 93:33; D&C 76:50–70). That joy, of course, comes only through the mercy and love of Christ, which allows us to come into the presence of God to receive the fulness of the Father. Elder Dallin H. Oaks said, "God's mercy is the only source of the ultimate and eternal joy, which restores every loss, dries

41

every tear, and erases every pain. Eternal joy transcends all suffering."[20]

Alma is an example of one who felt eternal joy overcome suffering. On the one hand, his sins caused him to be "tormented with the pains of hell" (Alma 36:13) and "racked, even with the pains of a damned soul" (Alma 36:16). On the other hand, the Atonement of the Messiah replaced the bitter, intense pain of sin with the sweet joy of redemption.

In Alma's words, "Oh, what joy, and what marvelous light I did behold; yea, my soul was filled with joy as exceeding as was my pain!" (Alma 36:20). We all make mistakes and we all can repent. Therefore, we all can get glimpses of that joy Alma described if we will sincerely repent of our sins—be they big or small—as he did.

We are children of a loving God, and because he loves us so much he wants us to be happy. He designed the plan of happiness for us. It is not the "plan of rules, restrictions, and hoops that we must jump through so that we can eventually be happy," but the plan to find happiness and joy now and in the future. We are not wrong to strive to achieve the measure of our creation. We are not wrong to search for joy. By following God, we can find lasting joy and, like the people of Nephi, live "after the manner of happiness" (2 Nephi 5:27).

CHAPTER FOUR STEPS

1. Pray for confirmation that the Lord wants you to be happy and have joy even in the midst of difficult times.
2. Live the gospel to the best of your ability, since it is the way to happiness. As you do this, your capacity to live the gospel will grow.
3. Set aside five minutes every night to make a list of things you are grateful for. Make it specific to that day (like on a cold, snowy day you are grateful for a warm coat and gloves). Try not to duplicate previous lists. After two weeks of doing this consistently, you should notice a difference in how you feel.
4. Say one prayer a day just to thank Heavenly Father.
5. Send thank you notes, not just for gifts, but also for things people do for you. Not only will this foster gratitude in your life, but it will lift others' lives as well.
6. Practice saying positive things. Find some way to remind yourself, like putting a coin in your shoe, tilting a picture on the wall so it hangs crooked, or a note on the fridge. Then every time you see or

feel that thing it can remind you to say something positive. Say more positive than negative things.

7. Match the time you spend exposed to negativity (watching the news, reading the newspaper) with positive interactions (reading scriptures, spending quality time with loved ones). Give positive influences at least equal time in your life.

8. Try to enjoy the "dailiness of living." Practice being in the moment by focusing on a sense or feeling for the day. For example, "Today I am just going to notice the beauty of the world around me," or "Today I am going to focus on the delight of my child's smile."

9. Take time to enjoy your relationships with others. If you have children, take time to play with them. Avoid distractions and focus your complete attention on your spouse or a friend for a time.

10. Smile more.

NOTES

1. Joseph Fielding Smith, *Teachings of the Prophet Joseph Smith* (Salt Lake City: Deseret Book, 1938), 255–56.
2. Randy L. Bott, "Overcoming Spiritual Schizophrenia," Northridge Stake Conference in Orem, Utah, Nov. 9, 2002.
3. Glenn L. Pace, "They're Not Really Happy," *Ensign*, Nov. 1987, 39.
4. Ezra Taft Benson, "Mighty Change of Heart," *Ensign*, Oct. 1989, 2.
5. Seligman, *Authentic Happiness*, 56.
6. Hugh Nibley, *Collected Works of Hugh Nibley*, 3rd edition, (Salt Lake City: Deseret Book, 1987), 3:266.
7. Ezra Taft Benson, *Teachings of Ezra Taft Benson* (Salt Lake City: Bookcraft, 1988), 393.
8. Sterling W. Sill, in Conference Report, Oct. 1956, 63.
9. Elaine L. Jack, "Get a Life," *Ensign*, July 1995, 49.
10. Paul H. Dunn, "By Faith and Hope, All Things Are Fulfilled," *Ensign*, May 1987, 73.
11. Joseph F. Smith and John A. Widtsoe, comps., *Gospel Doctrine* (Salt Lake City: Deseret Book, 1919), 155.
12. Neal A. Maxwell, "Be of Good Cheer," *Ensign*, Nov. 1982, 66.
13. Benson, *The Teachings of Ezra Taft Benson*, 401.
14. Seligman, *Authentic Happiness*, 83.
15. Elaine L. Jack, "Get a Life," *Ensign*, July 1995, 49.
16. Wallis, "The New Science of Happiness," Feb. 21, 2005, *Time*, online at www.time.com.

17. Ibid.

18. Gordon B. Hinckley, *Way to Be!* (New York: Simon & Schuster, 2002), 18.

19. Quoted in Henry B. Eyring, "Remembrance and Gratitude," *Ensign*, Nov. 1989, 11.

20. Dallin H. Oaks, "Joy and Mercy," *Ensign*, Nov. 1991, 73.

CHAPTER FIVE

Live on Purpose

WHERE ARE YOU GOING?

In Lewis Carroll's classic, *Alice's Adventures in Wonderland*, Alice comes to a crossroads. As she stands in indecision, unsure of which path to take, she turns to the Cheshire cat and asks him which way she ought to go. The cat answers that it depends on where she wants to go. If you do not know where you want to go, it doesn't matter which path you take.[1] To determine which path to take in life, we first need to know where we want to go. If that destination remains elusive, as was the case with Alice, the direction of your life won't really matter.

Basic algebra teaches that you only need two things to go from one location to another. You need to know where you start (point A) and where you want to end (point B). Then you merely draw a straight line from A to B. However, as you advance further in math—calculus, for example—you discover that often it is not only necessary to have point A and point B, but you must also know what is happening before A, between A and B, and after B. It is this complete knowledge that allows you to plot a more accurate path.

In real life, a straight line from A to B will get you to your destination if you are walking across the backyard, but greater distances are usually more complex. For instance, my son's elementary school is half a mile southeast of my house. But in order to actually get from my house (point A) to the school (point B), I must first go south for a block, then turn east for half a block, stop, continue east for three more blocks, turn south again and travel on a road that first curves eastward and then westward, pass through a four-way stop, and then travel south a couple more blocks until finally arriving at school. All in all, the half-mile distance between point A and point B, in reality, takes nearly a mile to travel by minivan and is a far cry from a straight line.

In life, as well as math, what happens between A and B is rarely a straight line. When you delve deeper, what happens before, between, and after A and B is of paramount importance. Throughout history, philosophers and non-philosophers alike have tried to answer the questions "Where did we come from?" "Why are we here?" and "Where are we going?" Humankind has always searched for the more complete knowledge of what comes before mortal birth, what happens after mortal death, and what we should do in between the two.

As we move closer to the Savior's Second Coming, the number of natural and human-caused disasters is increasing. Paralleling that is a rise in people looking for some spiritual direction. Unfortunately, spiritual direction can be hard to find amid the worldly confusion regarding the nature of God, his teachings, and the purpose of life.

Satan has been very effective in causing people to either ignore the true purpose of life or to look in the wrong places for it. Elder Richard G. Scott warns, "The vast majority of Father's children have not only forgotten their Father in Heaven and the purpose of mortal life, but they rarely even think of Him nor ponder for what purpose they are here in mortality. They have been led to be absorbed by mundane things that distract them from the essential ones."[2] People are "tossed to and fro" (Ephesians 4:14) as they search for meaning and purpose in the tumult of today's world.

Without purpose we just let life happen, allowing ourselves to be swept along with whatever it throws our way. This is not really living, however; it's being lived. A person's life is already an expression of their purpose, whether consciously or subconsciously. Do you want your purpose to be decided by default? A clear understanding of life's purpose helps us choose to act instead of merely react to circumstances and challenges—we can act for ourselves and not be acted upon (2 Nephi 2:26).

As Latter-day Saints we recognize the Lord's plan for us and are blessed not only to know where we want to go, but where we came from and why we are here. In "The Family: A Proclamation to the World," the First Presidency and Quorum of the Twelve Apostles declare, "In the premortal realm, spirit sons and daughters knew and worshiped God as their

Eternal Father and accepted His plan by which His children could obtain a physical body and gain earthly experience to progress toward perfection and ultimately realize his or her divine destiny as an heir of eternal life."[3] The gospel of Jesus Christ reveals the entire meaning and purpose of life, not just point A and point B, but the important complete knowledge of what happens before, between, and after, as well.

The knowledge that our lives have purpose is built logically and masterfully on the fact that we are beloved children of God and that he wants us to be happy and have joy. If you understand how precious and how loved you are by your Father in Heaven, then it only makes sense that he would design a plan of happiness specifically for you. And he wants us not only to have joy at the culmination of his plan, but also along the way.

These marvelous truths shed an invigorating and resplendent light on our life here on earth. Would a perfect, loving, all-powerful father send you to earth unless it was important or necessary? Would any loving earthly father put his beloved child through such hardship needlessly? When we know our place in our Heavenly Father's heart, then it reasonably follows that an all-knowing and loving Heavenly Father sent us to mortality because it is absolutely necessary for our happiness.

Not long ago my son was asking questions about exactly why we have to come to Earth to be tested. I explained using a basketball analogy. Let's say you want to play basketball. So, you read books on basketball, listen to those who play the game, and study the good players. Soon you know all about the rules of the game, the techniques that work, and what you need to do to be really good at it. But if you never actually shoot a ball or practice, you will never be able to play. Some things, like expanding our character and becoming like God, are like basketball: you have to actually do it in order to learn it. We cannot learn what we must in this life unless we actually live it.

Through revelation we know that a war was fought in the premortal life for the chance to fulfill our purpose in life (Revelation 12:7–11; Moses 4:3). Furthermore, we know that this purpose can only be fulfilled through the exercise of agency in a testing ground. Elder Bruce R. McConkie wrote:

> In this mortal probation it is the design and purpose of the Lord to test us: to see if we will believe in him and obey his laws now that we no longer dwell in his presence, hear his voice, and see his face. He already knows how we respond—what we believe and how we act—when we

walk by sight. Now he is testing our devotion to him when we walk by faith: when his presence is veiled, his voice is afar off, and his face is seen by few men only.[4]

The Prophet Joseph Smith said that the plan of salvation should "be regarded as one of heaven's best gifts to mankind."[5] It fills the void of complete knowledge we need to succeed spiritually in this mortal existence. Trying to comprehend the trials and meaning of this life without understanding Heavenly Father's plan of salvation is like trying to understand a suspense novel by only reading the middle section.

Knowing the meaning, purpose, and ultimate direction of life helps us to face the trials of mortality with an eternal perspective. Instead of railing against the unfairness of life, we can actually feel grateful for tribulations as valuable learning experiences. As Spencer W. Kimball said, "Is there not wisdom in [God] giving us trials that we might rise above them, responsibilities that we might achieve, work to harden our muscles, sorrows to try our souls? Are we not exposed to temptations to test our strength, sickness that we might learn patience, death that we might be immortalized and glorified?"[6] We can ask ourselves what we can learn from each situation. Knowing where you are going makes it so that you have a purpose that is bigger than the problems or trials you may be facing at the moment.

In modern revelation the Lord has told us, "If you keep my commandments and endure to the end you shall have eternal life, which gift is the greatest of all the gifts of God" (D&C 14:7). And in John, we are told, "And this is life eternal, that they might know thee the only true God, and Jesus Christ whom thou hast sent" (John 17:3). Therefore, the purpose of mortal life is to prepare for eternal life, and we do that by coming to know God and his Son, Jesus Christ. As we come to know God and draw nearer to him, we will be able to feel more of that fulness of joy which is his, the culmination of which is eternal life.

We know we are beloved children of God and that he loves us deeply. Out of his profound love, our Heavenly Father has provided a way for us to achieve ultimate joy and happiness, just as any parent would wish for their child. This way is the plan of salvation, or "the great plan of happiness" (Alma 42:8). It is through following this plan that we not only come to know God but become more like him.

Just as we can only have a glimmer of comprehension of the true majesty and glory of God, we may only be able to slightly understand what awaits us at the end of this journey through the plan of salvation, since even the lowest glory—that of the telestial kingdom—"surpasses all understanding" (D&C 76:89). At times we may only be able to echo Nephi when he said, "I know that [God] loveth his children: nevertheless, I do not know the meaning of all things" (1 Nephi 11:17). We just need to trust our Father when he tells us that this life is for our good, that the trials are necessary, and that he truly will share "all that he hath" (D&C 84:38). We may have to rely on the fact that he knows what he is doing, even if we don't.

Elder Richard G. Scott taught that our joy in life depends on our trust in Heavenly Father and his holy Son, and in our conviction that their plan of happiness truly can bring us joy. He says, "A pebble held close to the eye appears to be a gigantic obstacle. Cast on the ground, it is seen in perspective. Likewise, problems or trials in our lives need to be viewed in the perspective of scriptural doctrine. Otherwise they can easily overtake our vision, absorb our energy, and deprive us of the joy and beauty the Lord intends us to receive here on earth."[7]

My mother tells of a field trip she once took with her college geology class to a desert in the Four Corners area. She remembers that the view was spectacular, and at one point she stood on the crest of a petrified sand dune, gazing with awe and wonder at the panoramic vista before her. When she turned to share with the others her appreciation of the beauty of God's creation, she faced a sea of backsides as everyone else knelt on the ground, faces pressed to the dirt, looking through handheld microscopes. Her classmates were so busy scrutinizing individual grains of sand that they completely missed the breathtaking beauty surrounding them. My mother returned home, noting with irony that the others couldn't see the gorgeous desert for the particles of sand.

THE GOOD NEWS: IT REALLY *IS* GOOD NEWS

The word *gospel* literally means "glad tidings" or "good news." But the gospel is not just any kind of good news. If you received the news that you inherited a large sum of money, that would be good news, but it would not be the gospel. The gospel is a particular kind of good news: the best news!

The gospel is the good news of comfort to those like Moroni, the last surviving Nephite, who must struggle alone. It is the good news of reassurance to those like Jairus, who mourn the loss of a loved one. It is the good news of loving mercy for those like Alma, who feel they are eternally shackled by the consequences of sin. It is the good news of spiritual cleansing for those like the people of King Benjamin who are weighed down by godly sorrow at falling short of what they want to be. It is the good news of peace and strength to those like the people of Limhi, who live righteously but still suffer burdens placed on them by circumstances or by other people.

King Benjamin told his people that the gospel is powerful, great news: "And moreover, I would desire that ye should consider on the blessed and happy state of those that keep the commandments of God. For behold, they are blessed in all things, both temporal and spiritual; and if they hold out faithful to the end they are received into heaven, that thereby they may dwell with God in a state of never-ending happiness" (Mosiah 2:41).

You see, the gospel really *is* good news. Yet too many of us tread water in the gospel sea, half-heartedly dog-paddling here and there without ever finding true rest for our souls. The Church and its teachings are more than guidelines to follow in order to live a pretty good life. This is the only true Church of the living God, and only through the teachings found in his gospel can we understand the true purpose of life and come to know God the Father and his Son, Jesus Christ, a knowledge that infuses us with gratitude and joy.

VISION

Victor Frankl was a Jewish-Austrian psychiatrist who was interned in a Nazi concentration camp during World War II. He lost his wife and family, yet he emerged from his horrifying experience in triumph. From his experience, Frankl was convinced that man's deepest desire is to search for meaning and purpose, which was in stark contrast with other philosophies at that time. He observed that many of the concentration camp prisoners died when undergoing less hardship and suffering than those who survived. The survivors tended to be people who envisioned a future for themselves despite their present suffering, people who believed there was a deeper meaning in life and did not surrender to despair.[8]

Those survivors focused beyond the horrors of their current situation to a far better circumstance and outcome. They had vision. Vision is not merely just seeing with our eyes, but the way that we look at things—our perception. Understanding our purpose in life helps to clarify and focus our vision.

In the business world, there is a heavy emphasis on corporate vision. This is usually achieved using workshops and seminars to distill the overall vision into a tangible mission statement. The purpose of a mission statement is to clarify the desired end: what the corporation will become and what they will do to become that. A vision is not just a goal (like achieving a certain revenue), but an indicator of direction that helps keep the company on track and focused on where it is heading.

Stephen R. Covey, author of *The 7 Habits of Highly Effective People,* writes about the importance of determining your own vision. An individual vision "becomes a personal constitution, the basis for making major, life-directing decisions, the basis for making daily decisions in the midst of the circumstances and emotions that affect our lives. It empowers individuals with the same timeless strength in the midst of change."[9]

Self-improvement experts say that a written mission statement gives more power and incentive to carry on than merely wanting or desiring a certain outcome. When my brother entered the Missionary Training Center, all the new missionaries were asked to write a personal mission statement. They were advised to read it daily while out in the mission field. If it works for missionaries, then why not for mothers, fathers, visiting and home teachers, or ward members?

Interestingly, the leaders of our Church use mission statements all the time. The Young Women stand and repeat every Sunday what could be considered a mission statement. The Relief Society declaration could also be considered one, and the proclamation on the family without a doubt helps us make decisions. You could also consider your patriarchal blessing as a mission statement for your own life, given to you by God through inspiration.

Motivational speaker Wendy Hearn states, "The one thing I've noticed in my work is that very few individuals or [organizations] really harness the power generated by a strong vision. Clear definition of your vision acts as a magnet to pull you forward in the direction you truly want to take. Your vision provides inspiration for you and, if communicated well to [others], inspires them too."[10]

Our Eternal Father knows the power of vision. Long ago, Solomon proclaimed, "Where there is no vision, the people perish" (Proverbs 29:18).

Then, during his mortal ministry, the Savior taught, "The light of the body is the eye: if therefore thine eye be single, thy whole body shall be full of light" (Matthew 6:22). And what better statement of vision is there than Captain Moroni's title of liberty, which inspired a nation to fight for what was truly important (Alma 46:11–13, 19–21)? Sheri L. Dew suggests that "the mortal experience is largely about vision."[11] A vision of who we are and can become, of our individual worth, and of the critical role we play in these latter days is vital to our spiritual survival.

When someone "catches the vision" of something, they become excited and invigorated. Once we truly catch the eternal vision, it will show in our lives and countenances. It will flow from us and inspire others as well. We can be the visionary leaders of the world that our Heavenly Father sent us to be, bestowed with discernment, perception, and foresight, because we are led by revelation from him.

INDIVIDUAL PURPOSE

The plan of salvation gives meaning and purpose to mortal life for all of God's children, but each of us also has a unique, individual role—even if we don't feel like we do. There will be times when you may look at your life and think, "Is this what I was born to do?" Is constantly cleaning up after messy kids, tending screaming babies, or arguing with wayward teenagers your grand calling in life? Is remaining single despite all attempts, or sitting through painful church lessons on family after yours has been shattered really part of the great plan of happiness? Is losing everything through financial hardships or forcing yourself to work every day in a job you hate really part of your life's purpose?

We all have times when these types of feelings and questions plague us. We can learn a lesson from the story of Esther, who may have felt that way also. After her parents passed away, Esther's cousin, Mordecai, took her in as his daughter. The king of the land became angry with his disobedient wife and began a search throughout the kingdom for a new queen. Beautiful women from all the provinces were brought to the palace, and Mordecai presented Esther to the king. She pleased the king, and he made her his queen.

After Esther became queen, the king's chief advisor, who hated Jews, persuaded the king to have all the Jews in the kingdom put to death. Realizing the grave danger that loomed over his people, Mordecai pled with Esther to seek help from the king. However, under punishment of death, no one—not even the queen—could enter the presence of the king uninvited.

Further complicating the matter, the king did not know Esther was a Jew. Even if she escaped death for entering his presence uninvited, the king would surely discover Esther was a Jew if she sued for mercy on their behalf. The only way to remain safe was to do nothing. Mordecai, however, encouraged Esther to do what she—and only she—could do. He said to her, "Who knoweth whether thou art come to the kingdom for such a time as this?" (Esther 4:14). Esther took courage and spoke to the king. She found favor with him and her people were saved.

Former general Relief Society president Mary Ellen Smoot testified, "The Spirit has borne witness to me that we each have been born 'for such a time as this' (Esther 4:14). . . . Like Esther, we must prepare for our time because our time has come."[12] You were saved to come to earth at this time. In the midst of the overwhelming details of mortal life, do not forget that you not only have purpose as one of God's children, but also as one of the Lord's army of righteous Saints. When you radiate enthusiasm as a righteous child of God, you will affect others for good in ways you cannot know, but the Lord does.

Finding individual purpose in life is a universal search, and we are not alone in yearning for a life of significance. God has a purpose for each of us—an individual plan for every one of his children within the plan of salvation. We can feel a peace and security through fulfilling our unique mission. To do this, we must live close to the Spirit (through prayer, study, and righteous living) in order to avoid distractions or selfish goals that might frustrate the Lord's design for us and cause us to forsake it.

Sometimes life changes and transitions can obscure our vision so that we lose sight of life's meaning and purpose. We must be careful not to align our entire purpose in life with a particular role, because many face a role crisis at some point in their lives. Perhaps this happens when people find themselves divorced and devoid of the role of spouse that used to define their lives. Many women face this crisis when they confront a life without children or when their children are grown. Men may have a crisis when they have to switch jobs, or if they face disability or illness that challenges their role as breadwinner. If we only feel a sense of purpose within a particular role, we can feel adrift when that role changes or ends.

No matter the role we are living, we are children of God with a divine purpose and destiny. If we let him, God can weave the threads of our life into the tapestry of his kingdom, with a beautiful design that we will be unable to appreciate until much later. Our ordinary routines and daily roles—no matter what they are—can provide incredible opportunities to help others become more like Christ. Perhaps what you are doing is something that no one else could do in quite the same way.

The world would have you think that you can only make a difference in large and grand ways, but the Almighty knows that we make a difference in small ways, and that we have great purpose. Marian Wright Edelman once said, "We must not, in trying to think about how we can make a big difference, ignore the small daily differences we can make which, over time, add up to big differences that we often cannot foresee."

When I met my husband, I thought I knew my purpose in life. Yes, I wanted to be a good LDS woman, but if I had written down my life's purpose, I would have listed at least a dozen things before anything even close to being a mom and raising a family showed up. I had homeless shelters to establish, award winning music videos to choreograph, and a variety of other grandiose plans to pursue. Now I know that all those good intentions would have eventually fallen short because they were not part of the Lord's plan for me—at least not yet. My greatest moments of joy have come when I was absolutely certain that what I wanted mirrored what the Lord wanted me to do. He clearly sees my purpose in his plan. I just have to let him show me.

When you know the complete knowledge and the purpose of your life, it is like a light being switched on. The knowledge illuminates everything you do, and even if you must strive after that purpose your entire life, you will not mind so much because you know what it is; you know the end goal. One person working with purpose has more power than ten people working without.

Your life has meaning: you are the child of a loving Heavenly Father who wants you to come home to him. Your life has purpose: you are here to be tested and show that you will be obedient, valiant, and true to your own choice, coming to know God and qualify for eternal life with him in the process. You can rejoice in the complete knowledge that gives meaning and purpose to everything you do and experience. And you will enjoy the journey as you live your life with purpose, on purpose.

CHAPTER FIVE STEPS

1. Read your patriarchal blessing often, viewing it as a mission statement.
2. Write your own mini mission statements for the church callings you receive, for your profession, for your family, and so forth.
3. Prayerfully consider goals and write them in your journal.
4. Don't sweat the small stuff. Keep your vision focused on the big picture (and allow others to as well).
5. Analyze your life for ruts. We all get in a rut—some better than others. Plan ways to break out of your current rut and progress to a better rut.
6. Brainstorm your purposes in life, both on a short-term and long-term basis. For example, one of my short-term purposes may be to make sure that my children feel loved each day, and a longer-term purpose could be to instill gospel habits in my children. Sit down at a computer or with a pad of paper and just start writing. By getting it out on paper, you can identify and clarify your purpose. Don't worry if some ideas are trivial or silly; the important ones will eventually come out. Then list the important ones separately. Look at it often.

NOTES

1. Lewis Carroll, *Alice's Adventures in Wonderland* (New York: Dover Publications, Inc., 1993), 41.
2. Richard G. Scott, "Truth Restored," *Ensign*, Nov. 2005, 78.
3. "The Family: A Proclamation to the World," *Ensign*, Nov. 1995, 102.
4. Bruce R. McConkie, *The Promised Messiah: The First Coming of Christ* (Salt Lake City: Deseret Book, 1978), 1:84.
5. Joseph Smith and B. H. Roberts, eds., *History of The Church of Jesus Christ of Latter-day Saints*, 2nd ed. (Salt Lake City: Deseret Book, 1980), 2:23.
6. Spencer W. Kimball, *Faith Precedes the Miracle* (Salt Lake City: Deseret Book, 1972), 97.
7. Scott, Richard G. "Finding Joy in Life," *Ensign*, May 1996, 24.
8. See Victor Frankl, *Man's Search for Meaning* (New York: Pocket Books, 1984).
9. Stephen R. Covey, *The 7 Habits of Highly Effective People* (New York: Simon & Schuster, 1989), 108.
10. Wendy Hearn, "Harness the Power of a Strong Vision," Business-Personal-Coaching, online at www.business-personal-coaching.com.

11. Sheri L. Dew, "This Is a Test. It Is Only a Test," *Ensign*, July 2000, 62.

12. Mary Ellen Smoot, "For Such a Time as This," *Ensign*, Nov. 1997, 86.

CHAPTER SIX

Clear Away the Clutter

SPRING CLEANING

All of us have at least one place where we stash our clutter—whether it's a junk drawer (or two), a closet, or an entire basement or garage devoted to "stuff." And if you are like many people, you somehow end up with all of the above. We usually just toss stuff in our junk areas, always with the intention to organize and clean it up later. However, as the demands of life keep us constantly busy, later rarely arrives. When we finally do get around to it, the clutter has often reached daunting proportions.

Our life, just like our basement, can become too cluttered. A cluttered life is a life that has somehow gotten out of your control. When the things you have surrounded yourself with—and allowed to use up your time—are controlling you and negatively influencing your happiness and eternal progress, then you know your life is too cluttered.

Numerous things can clutter our lives. The most obvious is material clutter, or the stuff we collect. Most people recognize the problems associated with material clutter. When I can no longer make it through the storage room without having to clamber around, over, and through an obstacle course, I know that it's time for some spring cleaning. You can easily find a host of products for organizing your stuff. There are television shows devoted to helping people create order out of their clutter chaos. You can even hire professional organizers these days.

Other things clutter the emotional, mental, and spiritual aspects of our life. This kind of clutter also slowly accumulates, sneaking up on us until it takes control of our lives without our realizing it. This lifestyle clutter, however, is much more damaging than material clutter, but many people do not think to spring clean their life. Surprisingly, a large step in enjoying the journey is not something you need to focus on, but figuring out which things you need to *stop* focusing on. You must spring clean your life.

BALANCE AND PRIORITIES

If you have too much stuff to begin with, then trying to organize your clutter often becomes merely moving it from one place to another. I have organized like this before. I will empty one box, only to divide up the same things into different boxes. In essence, though, I still have the same amount of clutter. I've just changed its location.

This is why professional organizers usually begin by throwing out some belongings. Interestingly, this essential first step is often the one that meets the most resistance. The professionals resort to coaxing, persuading, or bullying their clients into parting with possessions. It is amusing how far some will go to somehow keep their stuff. Many become surly and uncooperative, and others resort to hiding things or even convincing friends to "borrow" objects so that the owners can get them back later.

Although this rebellion is amusing, it is also sobering. Those who can't let go of their clutter in reality sabotage their own desires, and the attempt to organize adds more stress to their lives. Those who bite the bullet and actually part with their clutter find a sense of relief, more comfort in their living space, and often a greater appreciation for their remaining possessions. Ironically, the people who give up more in the beginning are better off in the end.

Similarly, it is difficult, if not impossible, to unclutter our emotional, social, and spiritual lifestyles with the idea that we just need to get things sorted and better organized. To clear away the clutter in your life, you have to choose which things must stay and which can be thrown out. Yet how many of us sabotage our own happiness by doggedly refusing to discard lifestyle clutter?

Professional organizers have their clients sift through all their possessions, choosing which ones to keep and which ones to discard. Frequently the organizers will make people go through the process multiple times until they discard enough clutter. We can also sift through our lives in a similar way, categorizing the different ways we choose to spend our time and energy, depending on how well they serve our end goals. To clear away the clutter we must prioritize.

We cannot just haphazardly prioritize and call it good, however. It is necessary to have our priorities aligned correctly. In the book of Jeremiah, Jehovah denounced mankind, saying, "My people have committed two evils; they have forsaken me the fountain of living waters, and hewed them out cisterns, broken cisterns, that can hold no water" (Jeremiah 2:13). Everyone thirsts for the living waters, even those who do not know they do. Unfortunately, many spend endless hours and precious strength digging their own wells looking for water when the cooling drink of the living waters of the Redeemer is within easy reach.

I have found myself digging my own wells at times in my life. When we had our first child, I consciously chose to stay home with him. I knew it was the right decision, but it was still difficult because I have always worked hard to be financially self-reliant. Even though my husband has been fortunate to earn enough money for our needs, deep down I struggled with the fact that I was not helping financially.

Over the years I searched various ways to make money and still be home with my young children. Most of the things I tried did not work. Some could have succeeded but took too much time away from my family. I spent precious time and energy on them, and the related stress cluttered my life. I felt overwhelmed and stretched thin so many times, yet I could not give up. I kept trying the next idea, only to stress more when it didn't work either.

There came a point when I realized that these feelings I was so stubbornly clinging to were actually impeding my enjoyment of life. I didn't have a bad desire, but it was sapping my energy and robbing me of serenity and happiness. I finally understood that I couldn't do it all, that I needed to focus on other things right now, and, more importantly, that it was okay. When I shifted my priorities, discarding the clutter that I had unconsciously been carrying around, a large weight fell from my shoulders.

It is dangerously easy to get so caught up in the ever-present details of life that, before we realize it, we are spending our strength digging wells and searching for water in the wrong places, even when we know better.Gospel scholar Brent L. Top reflected, "Numerous good and honorable causes beckon for our time and energy. Whether selfishly or unselfishly, we may get and spend, hurry and scurry, come and go, and later discover that we have laid waste our emotional and spiritual strength and given our hearts away to things that matter very little in the end."[1] There are so many things that we can spend our time and energy worrying about—even good things—that we can often feel weighed down and overwhelmed.

Part of aligning our priorities is balancing the different aspects of our lives. When we allow areas of our lives to become cluttered, our spiritual equilibrium is usually affected, causing us to feel out of balance. This feeling of imbalance is a built-in alert that you probably need to spring clean your life. If we let the things of the world crowd in, all too often the wrong things inch their way up to the top of our priority list. When that happens, we run the risk of forgetting the fundamentals, like who we are and why we are here. This distorts our vision, which then contributes to further misaligned priorities. Before we know it, we can be unsuspectingly caught in a vicious cycle.

The pace of life is becoming more and more frantic; thus it is important that we consciously, deliberately, and frequently reexamine our priorities. Our leaders counsel us to regularly think about where we are going in life and what we need to do to get there. Even the Savior often "withdrew himself into the wilderness, and prayed" (Luke 5:16). We need to rejuvenate ourselves spiritually as the Savior did.

A story in John underscores the importance of keeping our priorities aligned. You have probably heard the story of two sisters, Mary and Martha. Both women loved the Lord, and Jesus loved them (John 11:5). On one occasion Martha received Jesus into her house. As a good hostess, Martha was making dinner and, as the scripture says, "was cumbered about much serving" (Luke 10:40). In other words, she was busy, tired, and stressed!

Mary, on the other hand, "sat at Jesus' feet, and heard his word" (Luke 10:39). Martha became increasingly upset that no one was helping her. She turned to Jesus and said, "Lord, dost thou not care that my sister hath left me to serve alone? bid her therefore that she help me" (Luke 10:40).

The Lord's loving reply may have surprised her. He said, "Martha, Martha, thou art careful and troubled about many things: But one thing is needful: and Mary hath chosen that good part, which shall not be taken away from her" (Luke 10:41–42).

The story of Mary and Martha often leaves the reader feeling that somehow Mary is the spiritual one, while Martha is the practical one; that somehow Martha is not spiritually equal to her sister. In casual reading of the story we may mistakenly assume that Mary sat at Jesus' feet while Martha worked in the kitchen the whole time, but in Luke's account of the story we learn that Martha "*also* sat at Jesus' feet, and heard his word" (Luke 10:39; emphasis added). They *both* sat and listened to the words of the Lord—together.

As time passed, however, it appears that Martha, the caring hostess, wanted to show her love of the Savior by providing a meal for him. Wanting to serve the Lord a wonderful meal is by no means a bad decision, but was it the best decision at the time? Evelyn T. Marshall clarifies, "The question here is one of priorities. Even special meals can become too complicated if we spend hours frosting the petit fours instead of planning more simply-prepared food. Do we spend more time planning and executing a lavish Sunday dinner for family members than we do studying the scriptures that day? Do we value a perfectly clean home over spending time teaching and loving our children?"[2]

Elder Neal A. Maxwell warned, "When we get filled with Martha-like anxiety, it usually stems from failure to establish proper priorities."[3] I spent years being "careful and troubled" about my desire to bring in a little extra money. It may seem like a small stress to some, but, like Martha, I was cumbered about, and it skewed my priorities.

Sometimes we need to leave the laundry, ignore the mess, say no to work, or take a break from extracurricular activities in order to focus on the important things. The story of Mary and Martha, observes Elder Dallin H. Oaks, "reminds every Martha, male and female, that we should not be so occupied with what is routine and temporal that we fail to cherish the opportunities that are unique and spiritual."[4] One of the tests of this life is learning to make more Mary-like choices and have less Martha-like worries. We do that by spring cleaning our life and consciously choosing our priorities—priorities picked from the tree of life that are designed to bring us joy.

TIME MANAGEMENT

The difference between Mary-like choices and Martha-like choices can be considered in terms of time management. Many people think of time management only as improving productivity or accomplishing more in the same amount of time. However, time management is more about what we choose to do with our time, not just how much we can cram into each hour.

If you think about it, our life on Earth is a lesson in time management. We are sent here for a specific amount of time (our mortal probation) in which we must learn and progress in certain areas. If we do so, we will then be in a position to continue that growth and progression once this mortal time is up. Ultimately, Satan's end goal is to have us squander our time on Earth. He can do this through temptation, deception, or distraction. All Satan needs to do is have us manage our probationary time poorly.

Time thieves surround us. Contemporary studies report that from September 2004 to September 2005, the average American household watched television 8 hours and 11 minutes per day. This is almost double from the previous year and is the highest TV watching levels since tracking began in 1950.[5] That equals *four months a year* spent in front of the TV. I would guess that in many cases computer and video games approach—or even exceed—TV time. Just think what good and valuable things could have been done with that four months.

Knowing that you want to live worthily and be obedient, how might Satan endeavor to lead you from the path to happiness? He would most likely not successfully tempt you to commit serious transgression—at least not at first. Elder Richard G. Scott explains, "He [Satan] would more likely fill your mind and heart with visions of many, many worthwhile things, none of which could be criticized as being wrong, but taken together, would so occupy your time that you would not do those things that are absolutely essential for eternal life with Father in Heaven and his Beloved Son."[6]

One of the gurus of time management, Stephen R. Covey, stated that the essence of time management can be captured in a single phrase: Organize and execute around priorities.[7] So time management is essentially learning to prioritize, and then, more importantly, living according to those priorities.

" 'Time management,' " writes Covey, "is really a misnomer—the challenge is not to manage time, but to manage ourselves."[8] Covey asserts that those who struggle with time management usually do not have a problem with discipline. Rather, their basic problem is that their priorities simply have not become deeply planted in their hearts and minds.[9]

To sift through our lifestyle clutter and prioritize, we must first understand what the most important priorities are. Then we must deeply ingrain them into our hearts and minds. When that happens, the discipline to manage our time according to our priorities will follow.

With Martha and Mary, Jesus taught how to prioritize when facing limited amounts of time and energy. We must learn how to manage our time, because, as C. S. Lewis once said, "Our leisure, even our play, is a matter of serious concern. [That is because] there is no neutral ground in the universe: every square inch, every split second, is claimed by God and counterclaimed by Satan."[10]

FIRST AND FOREMOST

During the Savior's mortal ministry, a lawyer, thinking to trick Jesus, asked him, "Master, which is the great commandment in the law?" The Savior replied, "Thou shalt love the Lord thy God with all thy heart, and with all thy soul, and with all thy mind. This is the first and great commandment" (Matthew 22:35–38).

The first step to correctly aligning our priorities is putting God first. This seems like a simple idea, but in practice many find it difficult. It is amazing how subtly the adversary and the world can affect our priorities. Ezra Taft Benson taught:

> We must put God in the forefront of everything else in our lives. He must come first, just as He declares in the first of His Ten Commandments, "Thou shalt have no other gods before me" (Exodus 20:3).
>
> When we put God first, all other things fall into their proper place or drop out of our lives. Our love of the Lord will govern the claims for our affection, the demands on our time, the interests we pursue, and the order of our priorities.[11]

The first great commandment is to love the Lord, first with all our heart, then our soul and mind. The Lord needs our heart first, because that is where our desires reside. Satan is also after our hearts. If he can control our feelings and desires, he can control us. Ultimately you will become what you give your hearts to, because "it is what you do and what you think about that determine what you are and what you will become."[12]

In the end, everything depends on your desires, because these shape our thought patterns and behavior. The Lord tells us, "According to your desires . . . shall it be done unto you" (D&C 11:17), "for I, the Lord, will judge all men according to their works, according to the desire of their hearts" (D&C 137:9). No matter what you may say your priorities are, the truth really lies in how you spend your time.

We all struggle with stubborn desires that tend to distort our priorities away from the things of eternity. Many try to find a way to hold on to their desires and also give their hearts to God. This often results in a situation where we become double-minded. We attempt to do two conflicting things at once. Lot's wife struggled with this ambivalence, and even as she fled Sodom, part of her longed to remain. She tried to obey the Lord while still yearning after the things of Sodom, and this was her downfall (Genesis 19:26).

Some try to change their desires by changing their actions only, hoping that somehow their recalcitrant mind and heart will fall into line. However, until the desire is in the right place, the actions will not be as beneficial. The gospel requires us to dedicate our minds and hearts, as well as our hands. In fact, spiritual ambivalence can freeze and paralyze our progress.

Sometimes we must wrestle with inward desires in order to put our priorities where they should be, but remember that God has "ways of educating our desires."[13] Elder Maxwell taught that we can educate our desires only as we learn more about what God's desires for us are, and then we must trust him to desire what is best for us.[14] If we have confidence in the Lord's deep love for us, this will be easier to do.

Like those who turn to professional organizers for help, we can turn to those who know what they are doing to reduce our lifestyle clutter. It has always been the job of the Lord's prophets to urge followers to dispense with Babylonian clutter. Usually this can only be fully accomplished with heavenly help and guidance.

Some may inwardly struggle with the idea of putting God first because they believe deep down that their dreams or identities will get lost. These people mistakenly feel that somehow they must choose between the Savior and what they really want, or that they will lose themselves if they fully commit to God.

In *The Screwtape Letters*, C. S. Lewis talks about the idea found in the scripture, "He that findeth his life shall lose it: and he that loseth his life for my sake shall find it" (Matthew 10:39). Lewis writes, "When He talks of their losing their selves, He only means abandoning the clamour of self-will; once they have done that, He really gives them back all their personality, and boasts . . . that when they are wholly His they will be more themselves than ever."[15]

Despite what many feel, the issue is not choosing between God and ourselves or what we want. When we put God first, we organize our lives so that the important things of eternity are not sacrificed for worldly pursuits. Sometimes that means we must trust in the Lord's timing. When our souls become more allied with God, our desires alter and become more godlike.

You are then set free to be more yourself than ever. You are not abandoning your dreams in order to follow God. Instead, following God becomes your dream, and all the other things for which you might righteously wish will one day be added unto you (3 Nephi 13:33). That is where full happiness can be found. And ultimately, submitting our wills to God's is really the only thing that we can give him that he didn't give us in the first place.

Putting God first can seem challenging when you are living in the middle of a world intent on capturing your desires. Yet when we finally commit to it, things are actually easier. President Brigham Young explained:

> They who love and serve God with all their hearts rejoice evermore, pray without ceasing, and in everything give thanks; but they who try to serve God and still cling to the spirit of the world, have got on two yokes—the yoke of Jesus and the yoke of the devil, and they will have plenty to do. They will have a warfare inside and outside, and the labor will be very galling, for they are directly in opposition one to the other. Cast off the yoke of the enemy, and put on the yoke of Christ, and you will say that his yoke is easy and his burden is light.[16]

Only through aligning our wills with the Lord can we know him better, become more like him, and have true joy. Everything else is just clutter, blocking us from the joy and happiness our Eternal Father plans for us.

Clear away the clutter. Spring clean your life. Learn to say no to those things that can cause the misuse and underuse of your time and talent.

We can be pulled in multiple directions by many good things, but we must, like Mary, decide what is most needful at that time in our life. We cannot always accomplish everything we want all at the same time, despite what society claims. We must learn that there is a time and a season for different things in our lives and it is imperative that we focus on the needful things and let the clutter go. Then we will end up with more than an orderly house or yard. We will end up with more joy now, and receive a fulness of joy in the life to come.

CHAPTER SIX STEPS

1. Give the Lord equal time. We tend to give much more consideration every day to mundane, worldly matters. Make the time more balanced by giving the Lord more of your attention. One example is to read scriptures before reading a novel, getting on the computer, watching a ball game, and so forth.
2. Turn off the TV.
3. Work on uncluttering your Sabbath day. If you follow the Lord's guidelines for keeping the Sabbath day holy, you will find that spending time each week focusing mainly on spiritual matters will help your priorities align.
4. Track how you spend your time for one week. Then see if you are spending it wisely, in accordance with your top priorities. Change if you need to.
5. Pay your tithing before other bills.
6. Make a budget and stick to it. This may seem a strange goal, but a budget helps you differentiate between wants and needs. Needs are important. It is constantly trying to meet wants that clutters our life—both literally and figuratively.
7. Realize there is a time and season for things. Just because a young mom stays home with small children now does not mean she will never be able to pursue her desire for a career. Sometimes a desire should be shelved until later.
8. Think of times in your life when you followed the Lord's timing and can now look back and see how good that was. Write it down so you can reread it.
9. Be careful not to over schedule yourself or your family. If you are never able to eat a meal together or exchange more than a few words in a week, maybe it is time to cut back on some activities.
10. Brainstorm specific things that you can do in your life to put the Lord first. Then do it. One thing might be to read your scriptures first thing in the morning, before you do anything else.

NOTES

1. Brent L. Top, "A Balanced Life," *Ensign*, Apr. 2005, 26.
2. Evelyn T. Marshall, "Mary and Martha—Faithful Sisters, Devoted Disciples," *Ensign*, Jan. 1987, 28.
3. Neal A. Maxwell, *Deposition of a Disciple* (Salt Lake City: Deseret Book, 1976), 69.
4. Dallin H. Oaks, "Spirituality," *Ensign*, Nov. 1985, 61.
5. Nielsen Media Research, "Nielsen Reports Americans Watch TV at Record Levels," online at www.nielsenmedia.com.
6. Sarah Jane Weaver, "Keeping Commandments Guarantees Happiness," *Church News*, Aug. 30, 1997.
7. Covey, *The 7 Habits of Highly Successful People*, 149.
8. Ibid., 150.
9 Ibid., 157–58.
10. Quoted in Jeffrey R. Holland, "Sanctify Yourselves," *Ensign*, Nov. 2000, 38.
11. Ezra Taft Benson, "The Great Commandment—Love the Lord," *Ensign*, May 1988, 4.
12. Richard G. Scott, "The Sustaining Power of Faith in Times of Uncertainty and Testing," *Ensign*, May 2003, 75.
13. Smith, *Gospel Doctrine*, 297.
14. Maxwell, *That Ye May Believe*, 112.
15. C. S. Lewis, *The Screwtape Letters* (San Francisco: HarperCollins Publishers, 2001), 65.
16. Asa Calkin, ed., *Journal of Discourses* (Liverpool: 1854–56), 16:123.

CHAPTER SEVEN

Choose Good Companions

AUTHOR VICTOR L. LUDLOW tells the story of a Viking chieftain who wanted to reward his warriors after a particularly successful trading voyage. Each man was allowed to take whatever he wanted from the chieftain's storehouse. The only condition was that he had to carry it home by himself. The storehouse was filled with all manner of precious objects, and all the men but one quickly selected large loads of goods to carry home. The exception—one of the biggest, strongest warriors—selected the smallest, least costly item: a key to the storehouse. Regular, wise use of the key helped him accumulate abundant wealth, which he used to build his community. A few years later the elders elected this man to be their next chieftain.[1] Sometimes a seemingly small, simple gift can be the key to many blessings.

If our Eternal Father were also to allow each of his beloved children to choose gifts from his spiritual storehouse, many would probably act similar to the Viking warriors in the story, choosing grand and outwardly impressive spiritual powers. The most precious gift in the spiritual store-house, however, is so simple that it could easily be overlooked, and, just like the key to the chieftain's storehouse, it can also provide future access to all other spiritual gifts. This key gift is the constant companionship of the Holy Ghost.

After baptism we are all given what President Wilford Woodruff called the greatest gift we can receive in mortality.[2] When the gift of the Holy Ghost is bestowed upon us, we receive the privilege of being brought back into the presence of one of the Godhead. Just think, this marvelous gift allows us to be in companionship with a God! We can walk and talk with one, even as Adam walked and talked in the Garden of Eden with his Heavenly Father. We can literally be in the presence of God and "always immersed in the light and power of Godliness."[3]

The Holy Ghost is also the source of testimony and spiritual gifts. It enlightens our minds, fills our souls with joy, teaches us all things, and brings forgotten knowledge to our remembrance (John 14:26). The Holy Ghost also "will show unto you all things what ye should do" (2 Nephi 32:5).

Parley P. Pratt gave many more reasons why the Holy Ghost is so precious:

> The gift of the Holy Ghost . . . quickens all the intellectual faculties, increases, enlarges, expands and purifies all the natural passions and affections; and adapts them, by the gift of wisdom, to their lawful use. It inspires, develops, cultivates and matures all the fine-toned sympathies, joys, tastes, kindred feelings and affections of our nature. It inspires virtue, kindness, goodness, tenderness, gentleness and charity. It develops beauty of person, form, and features. It tends to health, vigor, animation and social feeling. It develops and invigorates all the faculties of the physical and intellectual man. It strengthens, invigorates, and gives tone to the nerves. In short, it is, as it were, marrow to the bone, joy to the heart, light to the eyes, music to the ears, and life to the whole being.[4]

What a marvelous gift! What a great manifestation of how important we are to God. How much he must truly love us.

AS A COMPANION

The gift of the Holy Ghost gives us the chance to always have him with us, just like missionary companions are together all the time. The opportunity to have him accompany us throughout our daily lives is not just the privilege of those who have never made mistakes, who are in leadership positions, or who have reached a certain lofty point of righteousness. We all can have the Holy Ghost as a companion.

We consider those we regularly associate with as companions, but you could also call the things we surround ourselves with our companions as well. How many have the TV as a companion? The computer? Worldly preoccupations? While these potential companions may relax us, amuse us, or spark interesting conversation, they may also waste huge amounts of time, dull our senses, and drive away the Spirit. President Faust remembered a song his grandfather used to sing that said, "Show me your companions, and I will tell you what you are."

Our companions truly are a window to our lives, so we want to choose companions that inspire us, protect us, and offer good counsel. The Holy Ghost desires to be this kind of companion, but far too often we fail to invite his company and listen to his guidance. Maybe we just haven't made it a priority to learn how to listen, or we don't feel worthy. Perhaps we don't really believe the Lord will talk to us, or we don't recognize it when he does. And perhaps we have just allowed the Spirit to be crowded out of our lives.

At the beginning of my quest to find greater joy in life, I tried different solutions given by the wisdom of the world. Subconsciously, however, I was unsurprised by my lack of progress. I had a gut feeling (perhaps prompted by the Holy Ghost) that these things wouldn't work. Deep down I knew the root cause of my unhappiness was due to a malnourished spirit.

Joy that is not a temporary emotional high, but a habitual inner joy, is learned from long experience with and trust in God. That experience comes through his Holy Spirit. Paul made it clear that it is "the spirit [that] giveth life" (2 Corinthians 3:6). Elder Marcus B. Nash said, "In order to have joy, you need to understand that, as a child of your Heavenly Father, you inherited divine traits and spiritual needs—and just like a fish needs water, you need the gospel and the companionship of the Holy Ghost to be truly, deeply happy."[5]

Throughout my life I have had occasional spiritual experiences that shine brilliantly in my memory, but far too often I seem content to camp out on some kind of spiritual plateau. I believe now that the concept of a plateau in our spiritual progression is misleading. Like many, I used to view spiritual growth like climbing stairs. We believe that we can make great leaps of spiritual growth and then take a break on the landing, catching our breath, regaining our strength, and resting on our laurels until we climb the next set of stairs.

However, in matters of the Spirit, I have come to realize that you are always moving, and there are only two directions—up or down. You cannot stay at a spiritually level state. This misconception that you can coast lures us into one of Satan's traps: "And others will he pacify, and lull them away into carnal security, that they will say: All is well in Zion; yea,

Zion prospereth, all is well—and thus the devil cheateth their souls, and leadeth them away carefully down to hell" (2 Nephi 28:21). If we are content to remain on a spiritual plateau, isn't that just like saying all is well?

The truth is that if we think we are just maintaining the same spiritual level, we are usually slowly sliding backward. If we are not consciously working to move up, we will move down by default.

It's like climbing a large sand dune. If you have tried it, you know what I'm talking about. The surface of the hill is still, until you set foot on it and disrupt its precarious equilibrium. Then the sand starts rolling down the hill, including what you are standing on, and you start to slide. You have to keep climbing in order to make any headway, because when you stop going up, you slowly, inexorably slide down the hill. You can make it to the top, but it takes constant, hard work.

The many times I thought I was staying on a certain level spiritually, I was really sliding farther from my Heavenly Father, and I didn't notice it until my spirit cried loud enough for help. I had chosen so many other companions that there was little room left for the Holy Ghost. I have no doubt that the level of peace and joy I experience is closely correlated to the amount of space—in terms of both breadth and depth—that I make for the Spirit in my life.

HOW THE SPIRIT SPEAKS TO US

Elder Neal A. Maxwell lamented, "Members of the Church have received the gift of the Holy Ghost, but in many it lies dormant."[6] The problem in effectively using the gift of the Holy Ghost does not lie in our ability to receive revelation, because all those who are baptized and confirmed in The Church of Jesus Christ of Latter-day Saints are entitled to it. The first hurdle is living worthy enough so that the Holy Ghost can give us revelation. Remember, he is a part of the Godhead and is offended by sin and wickedness. Even if we are not actively participating in sin, if we allow it in our presence (on the TV or radio, for instance) the Spirit will not stay with us. The actual enjoyment of this precious gift is based on personal righteousness.

The second challenge is understanding the intended messages when we do receive promptings. Whenever a church lesson addresses the Holy Ghost, you almost always hear members remark on how hard it is to tell when they are actually prompted by the Spirit. It can be hard to differentiate between your own thoughts and the whispering of the still, small voice, but following the Spirit is critical because "there is a greater need for divine oversight in our lives today than ever before."[7] Surely Heavenly Father knows this. Yet many members feel that they don't have spiritual experiences.

In his *Ensign* article "Have I Received an Answer from the Spirit?" Jay E. Jensen writes, "Although the Spirit may be the most important aspect of our latter-day work, many of us do not know how it functions; too often we are worked upon by the Spirit and do not even know it (3 Nephi 9:20)."[8] We hear and read about spectacular spiritual experiences: Alma and the sons of Mosiah being visited by an angel, Daniel in the lion's den, and the prison crumbling and freeing Nephi and Lehi, to name a few. This may lead some to believe that if they haven't experienced something similar, then they haven't had a spiritual experience.

In fact, Boyd K. Packer tells us that strong, impressive spiritual experiences do not come to us frequently. "The Spirit does not get our attention by shouting or shaking us with a heavy hand," President Packer teaches, "rather it whispers. It caresses so gently that if we are preoccupied we may not feel it at all. . . . Occasionally it will press just firmly enough for us to pay heed. But most of the time, if we do not heed the gentle feeling, the Spirit will withdraw and wait until we come seeking and listening."[9]

Many people have had spiritual experiences, but because they don't understand how the Spirit works, they may not realize it. In the Doctrine and Covenants the Lord explained that revelation comes "in your mind and in your heart" (D&C 8:2–3). If the Lord spoke something to our mind we would probably describe it as thoughts. If he spoke to our heart we would probably call it feelings. But if the Lord usually communicates through the Holy Ghost by using thoughts and feelings, how do we discern between the constant stream of self-generated thoughts and feelings and those strategically placed by the Lord from time to time?

If our lives are full of noise, it will be difficult to identify the thoughts and feelings from the Lord. We understand that if we are constantly surrounded by sound, or "outer noise," it will be harder to hear the Spirit. But our lives can also be full of "inner noise" intentionally created by the adversary to smother the still, small voice of the Spirit through a swarm of loud, persistent, persuasive, and appealing voices.

Inner noise is generated by many things. We know that sin, anger, and contention create tremendous inner noise. Other sources are less apparent. Physical tiredness, stress, apathy, busyness, worry, and illness are not wrong in themselves, but nonetheless can contribute to inner clamor. Great rushes of emotion can also add to the din, like when we desperately desire something. Martin Harris wanted the 116 pages of translation from the Book of Mormon so much that he ignored the Lord's negative answer. After pestering Joseph Smith and the Lord, Martin finally got his desire, only to tragically lose those pages.

There are things that you can do to enhance your ability to hear, recognize, and follow the Spirit. Recognizing the voice of the Lord through the Holy Ghost is not a simple skill at first, but it can be honed and developed through knowledge and practice. Reducing the noise around you—inner and outer—is a vital step.

Studying the word of God and sincere prayer are sources of inner quiet and serenity. Increasing our own personal reverence, like sitting quietly and preparing for the covenant-making process offered during sacrament meeting, can also calm internal clamor. Finally, putting aside the cares of the world and the rush of our daily lives, and finding a quiet place and a quiet time to sit, ponder, reflect, and meditate on a regular basis will make a big difference in how well we hear the promptings of the Spirit.

Another step in learning to recognize the promptings of the Spirit is becoming more familiar with the Holy Ghost and how he works. The scriptures give many examples and recorded experiences with the Holy Spirit. This is a good time for him to communicate with us, when our minds are usually more in tune with spiritual matters. Through increasing our knowledge of the Spirit, we can learn *how* the Holy Ghost speaks to us.

The Holy Ghost communicates in many ways: speaking peace to our mind, causing our bosom to burn, telling us in our minds and our hearts, or coming as a voice in our mind. The Holy Ghost might lead us to do something, occupy our minds and press upon our feelings, constrain us from dangerous or improper things, give us thoughts or insights out of the blue, or clarify our perceptions.

A word often used in the scriptures to describe the communication of the Spirit is *enlightenment*, which means to give greater understanding. It is like having things go from blurry to clear, like focusing a camera lens or putting on glasses. When the Spirit is with us we can see everything better than before.

If we want to feel those enlightening moments, we need to take advantage of every chance we have to feel the Spirit. It requires work on our part. Sometimes we work by praying, because prayer is a form of work.[10] While the Church was in its infancy in the 1830s, there was great anxiety from the leaders to obtain inspiration through the Spirit (D&C 63, section heading). The Lord told them, "Ye receive the Spirit through prayer" (D&C 63:64).

Many times, however, prayer alone is not enough work. God gently admonished Oliver Cowdery for praying without doing the labor and preparation needed on his part. He said, "You have supposed that I would give it unto you, when you took no thought save it was to ask me" (D&C 9:7).

It is my experience that spiritual inspiration often comes in the very act of doing, and only rarely beforehand. When you must give a talk or lesson in church, you can think and meditate all you want, but often the inspiration comes when you are actually preparing or even presenting. Elder Marion G. Romney said, "While the Lord will magnify us in both subtle and dramatic ways, he can only guide our footsteps when we move our feet."[11]

Nephi taught this very concept when he and his brothers were attempting for the third time to get the brass plates from Laban. They had exhausted their own ideas and, in the case of Laman and Lemuel, exhausted their courage as well. Nephi was determined to obey, so he entered Jerusalem, trusting that the Lord would help. He said, "I was led by the Spirit, not knowing beforehand the things which I should do" (1 Nephi 4:6). In the very act of doing, the Spirit did not let him down. Nephi was able to not only get the brass plates but also bring Zoram to join them.

After we hear and recognize spiritual promptings, we must act upon them if we wish for revelation to continue. There are many times that I am not sure if something I have felt is a prompting from the Holy Spirit. Usually, I decide to act on the idea, because I feel it is better to follow an impulse that may just be my own thoughts than risk the loss of the Spirit by not obeying a true prompting.

In many such instances, days or even months down the road I look back on events and can see the Lord's hand in my actions as I followed those impulses. This helps strengthen my testimony, and I am more willing to make that phone call when someone's name pops into my head, or deliver that food when the idea suddenly comes to me. And the Lord is more willing to communicate with me through the Holy Ghost as well.

THE COMFORTER

In speaking to his apostles, the Savior reassured them that he would not leave them comfortless when he left them (John 14:18). He promised that he would send them "the Comforter, which is the Holy Ghost" (John 14:26). Not only does the Spirit enlighten our minds, but it also fills our souls with joy and comfort. As Sheri L. Dew stated, "No mortal comfort can duplicate that of the Comforter."[12]

In times of great hardship and pain, we know that we can turn to the Holy Ghost for comfort. Like most of us, I have had moments like these in my life. More often, though, I have needed the comfort that only the Comforter can give for less grandiose events. I need him when I feel disappointment in myself because I handle a situation poorly. Those times when, despite my knowledge of who I really am, I let the voices of the world make me feel inferior, I need him. I need the Comforter when something debasing, vulgar, or evil accidentally impresses itself on my mind and I just want it gone so that my spirit can feel good again. And I yearn for comfort when my heart aches for the hardships of others and it hurts so bad just watching them go through it.

In the Doctrine and Covenants, the Lord calls the gift of the Holy Ghost "the unspeakable gift" (D&C 121:26). In these perilous and fearful times, we need this unspeakable gift not only to guide and direct us, but also to give us peace. Christ said, "Peace I leave with you, my peace I give unto you: not as the world giveth, give I unto you. Let not your heart be troubled, neither let it be afraid" (John 14:27).

The peace that the Lord offers is not necessarily the peace that comes from an easy and trouble-free life. It is not the world's peace, which is usually the absence of disturbance or war, but the Lord's peace—the ability to be tranquil despite the storms that rage around you. Through the Comforter we can have peace when we allow the Savior to help bear our burdens. Psalms declares, "Cast thy burden upon the Lord, and he shall sustain thee" (55:22). Sustaining does not mean the Lord will necessarily take away our heavy loads, however.

The Lord sustained the faithful people of Alma with their burdens. Alma and his people had years of peace after fleeing from the wicked King Noah. Then they were brought into bondage to the Lamanites. There came a point when their afflictions were so great that the people began to pray mightily to God and poured out their hearts to him (Mosiah 24:10–12). The Lord then told them, "Lift up your heads and be of good comfort," and then he covenanted to "deliver them out of bondage" (Mosiah 24:13).

However, the Lord did not immediately fix their situation. First he eased the burdens that were put upon their shoulders (Mosiah 24:14). The Lord did not remove the burdens, but made them light and strengthened the people so they could bear up their burdens with ease (Mosiah 24:15).

Not many of us are in physical bondage like the people of Alma, but we all have burdens. Other words for burden are weight, load, strain, stress, care, responsibility, trouble, anxiety, hardship, and infirmity. How many of us do not feel weighed down with anxieties or cares? Do you ever feel stressed or troubled? These are very real burdens, and the Spirit can help us carry them. In fact, we are told to cast them on the Lord. As Elder Jeffrey R. Holland testifies, "The Savior's Atonement lifts from us not only the burden of our sins but also the burden of our disappointments and sorrows, our heartaches and our despair."[13]

A good friend of mine, whose children are grown, once told me about a time when some of her children were making dangerous, destructive choices. As a young mother, I could not imagine the burden of watching your beloved children choose a path that you knew would take them away from the Lord and lasting joy. When asked how she could take it, she said that it came to the point where she felt her heart could not bear it anymore. She went to the temple and in the pain and anguish of her soul, cried to the Lord to please help her with her load. She shared that even though the burden remained, she was strengthened to the point that she could then carry it.

The Savior pleads with us, "Take my yoke upon you, and learn of me; . . . and ye shall find rest unto your souls. For my yoke is easy, and my burden is light" (Matthew 11:29–30). The Lord's yoke is one where he shares our burdens. And through the Atonement, Christ is more qualified than anyone to do so.

It says in Alma:

> And he shall go forth, suffering pains and afflictions and temptations of every kind; and this that the word might be fulfilled which saith he will take upon him the pains and the sicknesses of his people.
>
> And he will take upon him death, that he may loose the bands of death which bind his people; and he will take upon him their infirmities, that his bowels may be filled with mercy, according to the flesh, that he may know according to the flesh how to succor his people according to their infirmities. (Alma 7:11–12)

Like my friend and the people of Alma, we too can cast our burdens at the Lord's feet, and he will help us to bear them. We are not supposed to do everything alone. Perhaps the Lord even gives us more than we can bear by ourselves so that we will have to turn to him. In the Book of Mormon we are told, "And if men come unto me I will show unto them their weakness. I give unto men weakness that they may be humble; and my grace is sufficient for all men that humble themselves before me; for if they humble themselves before me, and have faith in me, then will I make weak things become strong unto them" (Ether 12:27).

Even though our weaknesses encourage us to go to the Lord for help, we still have our agency and are required to make the first move. Then we must strive to be worthy of his Spirit's companionship so that he can help us, and he promises that his grace is sufficient for us (2 Corinthians 12:9). We are much stronger in this life when we are walking with God than when we are walking alone. Together, there will be nothing you cannot endure, be it cancer, the loss of a loved one, depression, a wayward family, or financial hardship.

A MIGHTY CHANGE OF HEART

From the book of Mosiah we learn that all mankind must be born again—born of God, changed, redeemed, and uplifted—to become the sons and daughters of God. "And thus they become new creatures; and unless they do this, they can in nowise inherit the kingdom of God" (Mosiah 27:25–26).

There is a natural birth and a spiritual birth. The natural birth causes us to leave premortal life and creates a natural man, but the natural man is an enemy to God (Mosiah 3:19). The spiritual birth comes next and "it is to die as pertaining to worldliness and carnality and to become a new creature *by the power of the Spirit.* It is to begin a new life, a life in which we bridle our passions and control our appetites, a life of righteousness, a spiritual life."[14]

Our spiritual rebirth begins in our hearts. After hearing King Benjamin's address, his people began the process of spiritual birth with a mighty change in their hearts. They had "no more disposition to do evil, but to do good continually" (Mosiah 5:2). A mighty change of heart does not mean that we will never sin again, but that we are now inclined to do good. Though we still have human weaknesses, we choose to put off the natural man and yield to the enticings of the Holy Spirit (Mosiah 3:19), and our fundamental natural preference is changed from carnal to spiritual.

Brother and Sister Bishop, who I have referred to before, can remember when they each changed their lives to follow the course they are on now. The specifics of what exactly happened don't matter, but they can pinpoint the turning experience—their own mighty change of heart. They both trace the joy that they have now back to that day.

This spiritual transformation is performed through the Holy Ghost. With a change of heart, the Holy Ghost assists us in becoming new men and women in Christ. This transformation is shown through our belief in Christ's words, our desires for righteousness, our good works, and even our very appearance. Those who are born again not only live a new life, but they also have a new father. Their new life is one of righteousness, and their new father is God. They become the sons of God, or, more particularly, they become the sons and daughters of Jesus Christ.[15]

Spiritual rebirth is not guaranteed after baptism, however. One can be a baptized member of the Church, having received the confirmation and gift of the Holy Ghost, and not have a mighty change of heart. We may attend church regularly but shrink from commitments and from seeking the personal spiritual rebirth that comes from yielding our hearts to God. Alma asked, "Have ye spiritually been born of God? Have ye received his image in your countenances? Have ye experienced this mighty change in your hearts?" (Alma 5:14). He was not speaking to new converts or investigators but to the members of the Church.

Elder Joseph B. Wirthlin explains that a glorious new spiritual dimension comes to light when we open our hearts to the refining influence of the Holy Ghost. We can know for ourselves "things of the Spirit that are choice, precious, and capable of enlarging the soul, expanding the mind, and filling the heart with inexpressible joy."[16] Until we choose to change our heart, we will miss some unique blessings in this life, and be in jeopardy of missing the most glorious blessings in the life to come.

SANCTIFYING POWER

The Lord said, "The Spirit enlighteneth every man [and every woman] . . . that hearkeneth to the voice of the Spirit. And every one that hearkeneth to the voice of the Spirit cometh unto God, even the Father" (D&C 84:46–47). The ultimate blessing of the Holy Ghost in our lives is the spiritual refinement of our souls, or a baptism by fire. The scriptures refer to the Lord's cleansing as a "refiner's fire" (Malachi 3:2; 3 Nephi 24:2; D&C 128:24). A refinery uses extreme heat to burn away impure particles, making the metal strong. Every one of God's children must pass through a spiritual refining process before entering his presence. This refiner's fire is a purification and sanctification process.

Sanctification means "to consecrate" or "to make holy." The Atonement of Jesus Christ allows Holy Ghost, through a baptism by fire, to sanctify each worthy individual. Sanctification is a gradual process. Elder Bruce R. McConkie emphasized, "Nobody is sanctified in an instant, suddenly. But if we keep the commandments and press forward with steadfastness after baptism, then degree by degree and step by step we sanctify our souls until that glorious day when we're qualified to go where God and angels are."[17] Sanctification can only happen with the continuous presence of the Holy Ghost in our lives—with his companionship. Irregular and sporadic attempts to seek out the Spirit won't be enough to sanctify us.

We begin the process of sanctification with a change of heart. Then, when we are sanctified by the Holy Ghost, we become a new person. We view ourselves and others differently. Our habits, desires, personality, and behaviors change. We assume goodwill, we give others the benefit of the doubt, we love our enemies, and we do good to them that abuse us. In short, we have a "perfect brightness of hope, and a love of God and of all men" (2 Nephi 31:20).

The Lord wants to direct us, comfort us, and refine us through his Spirit, but it is our choice whether or not we let him. Just as metal is purified by the refiner's fire, we become more like Christ as the desires and temptations of sin are rooted out of our hearts by the sanctifying power of the Holy Ghost. Anger will be replaced with love. Anxiety will be replaced with faith. And despair will be replaced with joy as we live worthy of the companionship of the Holy Ghost.

CHAPTER SEVEN STEPS

1. Set aside a time every day to "Be still" (D&C 101:16). When you are still you can learn to hear the still, small voice.
2. Work to reduce outer and inner noise in your life so that when thoughts and feelings come they are not drowned out.

3. Use the time of the sacrament each Sunday to increase your personal reverence.

4. Study the scriptures and pray with a pen and notebook in hand. Write down thoughts that come to you. You may be surprised at the inspiration from the Spirit. Recognize that a wandering of attention during scripture reading is not necessarily a lack of concentration but may be the Spirit giving you direction.

5. Pray for the guidance of the Holy Ghost. When you are confirmed you are instructed to receive the gift of the Holy Ghost. It is something that we have to actively do ourselves.

6. Keep track of times when you have followed the direction of the Holy Ghost (or think you have). Go back and look at your record and in retrospect you will be able to see many times that your actions were in accordance with the Spirit.

7. Keep the Sabbath day holy. If the only difference between our average Saturday and our Sunday is three hours of church and no lawnmowing, I would suggest that we are not really honoring the Sabbath as the Lord intended. Proper observance of the Sabbath day will work wonders on your ability to hear the Spirit.

NOTES

1. Victor L. Ludlow, *Principles and Practices of the Restored Gospel* (Salt Lake City: Deseret Book, 1992), 298.

2. Wilford Woodruff and G. Homer Durham, comps., *The Discourses of Wilford Woodruff* (Salt Lake City: Bookcraft, 1946), 5.

3. John A. Widtsoe, *A Rational Theology as Taught by The Church of Jesus Christ of Latter-day Saints* (Salt Lake City: Deseret Book, 1965), 79.

4. Parley P. Pratt, *Key to the Science of Theology*, 10th ed. (Salt Lake City: Deseret Book, 1948), 101.

5. Marcus B. Nash, "The Great Plan of Happiness," *Ensign*, Nov. 2006, 49.

6. Neal A. Maxwell, "The Holy Ghost: Glorifying Christ," *Ensign*, July 2002, 56.

7. James E. Faust, "The Gift of the Holy Ghost—A Sure Compass," *Ensign*, Apr. 1996, 2.

8. Jay E. Jensen, "Have I Received an Answer from the Spirit?" *Ensign*, Apr. 1989, 21.

9. Boyd K. Packer, "The Candle of the Lord," *Ensign*, Jan. 1983, 51.

10. Bible Dictionary, "prayer," 753.

11. Marion G. Romney, "The Basic Principles of Church Welfare," *Ensign*, May 1981, 90.
12. Sheri L. Dew, "We Are Not Alone," *Ensign*, Nov. 1998, 94.
13. Jeffrey R. Holland, "Broken Things to Mend," *Ensign*, May 2006, 69.
14. Bruce R. McConkie, *A New Witness for the Articles of Faith* (Salt Lake City: Deseret Book, 1985), 282; emphasis added.
15. McConkie, *A New Witness for the Articles of Faith*, 284.
16. Joseph B. Wirthlin, "The Unspeakable Gift," *Ensign*, May 2003, 26.
17. Rulon T. Burton, ed., "Sanctification: Perfection," *We Believe: Doctrines and Principles of The Church of Jesus Christ of Latter-day Saints* (Salt Lake City: Tabernacle Books, 1994).

CHAPTER EIGHT

Stay in Touch

I LEFT HOME FOR the first time when I went to college. I had been on vacations, school-related trips, and stayed with my dad (who lived in another state) before that, but at those times I packed a suitcase, stayed in a hotel or guest room, and returned home before too long. When I moved away I was anxious to be on my own, so I was surprised that I missed home once I was gone. During the first couple months, I spent as much on my long distance calling card as I did on rent. My student budget couldn't handle that, so I had to switch to letters and email, but I did what I could to stay in touch with my family. I found support, happiness, and joy in maintaining that connection.

We are all away from home because our true home is in the heavens above. Earth is only a temporary home, much like a college dorm. We are surrounded by our earthly things, our friends, and our mortal families, but a part of our soul knows that we are not really home. Just like I yearned to stay in touch while I was at college, we all long, deep down, to have a connection with home. And just like my mom relished each call home, our Father in Heaven does too. When we stay in touch with our heavenly home and family, we will likewise find joy.

CALL HOME

Prayer is the calling card for us to connect with our heavenly home, and we don't need to remember any numbers or wait for our roommate to hang up first before using it. Yet many of us do not use prayer like we could. In college I could talk for hours on the phone while the charges on my calling card racked up, but my prayers were often over and done in two minutes flat—if I managed to stay awake during them.

Envision that you are talking to one of your best friends. Chances are that one of the things that make this friend so special is that he or she listens to you and understands you. If an imperfect person can listen to you that well, just think how much better your perfect Father in Heaven can listen. Imagine how much he can care.

Our Heavenly Father constantly invites us to pray and talk to him. Throughout the scriptures are invitations such as, "Seek me diligently and ye shall find me; ask, and ye shall receive; knock, and it shall be opened unto you" (D&C 88:63) and "Pray always, and I will pour out my Spirit upon you, and great shall be your blessing" (D&C 19:38). Never do the scriptures instruct us not to pray, or to wait until God isn't quite so busy. He tells us to pray always. And he wouldn't make the invitation if he didn't intend to listen.

The Bible Dictionary says that as soon as we learn—and understand—our true relationship to God (that God is our Father and we are his children) then prayer becomes natural and instinctive on our part. In fact, many of the so-called difficulties about prayer arise from forgetting or not understanding this relationship.[1] If we see God as uninvolved or unapproachable, then it would be difficult to pray to him. It would be even more difficult if we viewed God as harsh or judgmental. Can you see how important it is to sincerely believe that you are a beloved son or daughter of a loving Heavenly Father?

If we trust in our Eternal Father's love for us, we can grow closer to him. We will want to pray, and one of the ways we draw closer to God is through prayer. It is an upward, self-renewing cycle. As long as we know how to pray—and do so—we need never be alone. Our Father in Heaven is *always* accessible through prayer.

Our Father knows how important it is for us to stay in touch with home. He implores us to pray, while the enemy of our souls belittles and derides it. The warning from 2 Nephi is true: "For if ye would hearken unto the Spirit which teacheth a man to pray ye would know that ye must pray; for the evil spirit teacheth not a man to pray, but teacheth him that he must not pray" (2 Nephi 32:8). As we have discussed before, knowing God is part of the joy of eternal life. How can we get to know him if we never talk to him?

The story of Daniel in the Old Testament shows how far Satan will go to stop us from praying. In Daniel's case, he would be thrown into a den of lions and *killed* if he prayed (Daniel 6). Talk about extreme! Even in a situation like that, however, Satan cannot stop us from praying, just as he couldn't stop Daniel.

Not only can we find greater joy through prayer as we communicate with our Father and catch glimpses of our true home, but prayer is also a conduit for spiritual power. Unfortunately, almost everyone becomes casual with their prayers at some point. When we do, we cut ourselves off from this essential source of strength and revelation. The interesting thing is that the less we pray, the less we feel like praying and the harder it is to draw from the power available through proper prayer.

If you feel that you are not tapping into the power of prayer, Elder Joseph B. Wirthlin suggests you reflect on the effectiveness of your prayers. "How close do you feel to your Heavenly Father? Do you feel that your prayers are answered? Do you feel that the time you spend in prayer enriches and uplifts your soul? Is there room for improvement?"[2]

I regret that far too often I have felt that the time I spent in prayer may have been better spent elsewhere. If you feel the same after praying as you do after vacuuming, then there is definitely need for improvement. There are four general areas that prophets and apostles have counseled us to work on to improve our prayers.

First, we need to make our prayers meaningful. President Hinckley observed, "The trouble with most of our prayers is that we give them as if we were picking up the telephone and ordering groceries—we place our order and hang up. We need to meditate, contemplate, think of what we are praying about and for and then speak to the Lord as one man speaketh to another."[3] Meaningful prayers take time.

Part of making prayers meaningful is making them specific. If we were to conduct a conversation the way many of us say our prayers (with large generalities), it would be a short and boring conversation. After I finished my first book, I sent it off to a publisher. We prayed every night as a family for months that it would get accepted. Then, one night my husband asked in family prayer that it would get accepted tomorrow. The next day I received a phone call from the publisher saying they wanted my book! Not all specific requests will be answered in quite so grand a manner, but we will draw closer to our Father in Heaven when we open our hearts enough to share our life with him specifically.

We must also pray frequently in order to develop a meaningful relationship with Heavenly Father. We do not speak to our friends only in times of great joy or tribulation and ignore them when life is normal. Likewise, our prayers can and should be focused on the practical, everyday struggles and delights of life. That is how a true relationship is built.

Second, we need to pray with faith. Without faith, prayer loses power; it is merely words. Sometimes we approach our Heavenly Father like a child who asks something of his or her parents, knowing they will refuse. Little children instinctively believe God listens to them, but often that conviction deteriorates over the years.

Most of us have experienced the faith of a child's prayer. When my oldest son was a toddler, we lost his most beloved possession: a tattered blanket. When the loss was discovered at bedtime, we frantically searched the house and car—with no luck—while my son cried inconsolably. Finally, we had our little boy say a prayer, asking Heavenly Father to help us find the special blanket. Not long after, we had the idea to call the grocery store where we had gone that day, and, to everyone's joy, a customer had found the blanket. I don't doubt the faithful prayer of that little boy carried weight in heaven.

Third, we need to have and exercise charity. The Book of Mormon teaches, "If ye turn away the needy, and the naked, and visit not the sick and afflicted, and impart of your substance, if ye have, to those who stand in need—I say unto you, if ye do not any of these things, behold, your prayer is vain, and availeth you nothing" (Alma 34:28).

Finally, reading the scriptures and praying are interconnected. It seems we need the knowledge of home we receive through the scriptures in order to turn the key to prayer. Elder Henry B. Eyring says:

> We can and must go often and carefully to the word of God. If we become casual in our study of the scriptures, we will become casual in our prayers.
>
> We may not cease to pray, but our prayers will become more repetitive, more mechanical, lacking real intent. Our hearts cannot be drawn out to a God we do not know, and the scriptures and the words of living prophets help us know Him. As we know Him better, we love Him more.[4]

Additionally, many times we can find answers to our own prayers in the scriptures. If we read the scriptures often we will become familiar with the stories and teachings. When the answer to one of our prayers can be found in the scriptures, the Spirit can more readily bring them to mind. The scriptures are the Lord's voice in print.

Prophets through the ages have emphasized the power of prayer, because through it we can fight evil. "We are not capable of overcoming Satan alone," writes Clyde J. Williams, "because he remembers the premortal existence, he may know things about us that even we do not yet understand. Therefore, we must pray continually for the sustaining help of our Heavenly Father in overcoming his influence and that of his followers."[5] And President Hinckley has said, "There is no power on earth like the power of prayer."[6]

LETTERS FROM HOME

President Hinckley speaks gratefully of a letter from home he received while having a spiritual crisis of sorts on his mission. It was early in his mission, and he was discouraged. The work was hard, and the people were not receptive. Then he received a letter from his father, who wrote, "Dear Gordon, I have your letter. . . . I have only one suggestion: Forget yourself and go to work."

The young Gordon B. Hinckley got on his knees and made a pledge to try and give himself unto the Lord. He remembers, "The whole world changed. The fog lifted. The sun began to shine in my life. I had a new interest. I saw the beauty of this land. I saw the greatness of the people. . . . Everything that has happened to me since that's been good I can trace to that decision."[7]

That letter from home was life-changing for President Hinckley. We too can have letters from home that may have as great an impact. The scriptures are our letters from our heavenly home, and they simultaneously help us stay in touch, do what's right, and fight evil.

In his dream of the tree of life, Lehi saw an iron rod leading through the mists of darkness, which Satan used to lead away the children of men. Later, Nephi explained that the iron rod "was the word of God; and whoso would hearken unto the word of God, and would hold fast unto it, they would never perish; neither could the temptations and the fiery darts of the adversary overpower them unto blindness, to lead them away to destruction" (1 Nephi 15:23–24).

President Benson instructed that "however diligent we may be in other areas, certain blessings are to be found only in the scriptures."[8] Not only will the word of God lead us to the joy found at the tree of life, but through it we can hold fast to the good, find the power to resist temptation, and be armed with the Spirit. The scriptures not only provide answers and guidance for daily life, but they are literally a spiritual weapon. President Harold B. Lee told us that "the most powerful weapons the Lord has given us against all that is evil are, by His own declarations, the plain, simple doctrines of salvation as found in the scriptures."[9]

Alma learned that "the word had a great tendency to lead the people to do that which was just—yea, it had had more powerful effect upon the minds of the people than the sword, or anything else, which had happened unto them" (Alma 31:5). We can only use the scriptures to effectively combat evil, however, if we train with them regularly. Otherwise, they will be unwieldy and awkward in our hands.

We may sometimes feel that the scriptures are mostly directed toward those who need a "spiritual overhaul." But, of course, some people don't need a complete overhaul. Maybe they need only to charge their spiritual batteries. The great thing about God's letters is that they not only help those needing a spiritual overhaul, but they also help those who just need recharging.

For example, the Book of Mormon prophet Jacob delivered an address to an audience where some had great sins and needed the spiritual overhaul of deep repentance. He also knew that many were pure in heart and needed only a battery charge. This eloquent prophet preached a sermon to both.

For those wanting to recharge their spiritual batteries, Jacob said:

> Look unto God with firmness of mind, and pray unto him with exceeding faith, and he will console you in your afflictions, and he will plead your cause, and send down justice upon those who seek your destruction.
>
> O all ye that are pure in heart, lift up your heads and receive the pleasing word of God, and feast upon his love; for ye may, if your minds are firm, forever. (Jacob 3:1–2)

For those needing a spiritual overhaul, Jacob said:

> But, wo, wo, unto you that are not pure in heart. . . .
>
> Hearken unto my words; arouse the faculties of your souls; shake yourselves that ye may awake from the slumber of death; and loose yourselves from the pains of hell that ye may not become angels to the devil, to be cast into that lake of fire and brimstone which is the second death. (Jacob 3:3, 11)

Jacob's counsel to both groups was to listen to the word of God. For the pure in heart it was "the pleasing word of God," and for the sinners it was a warning to listen . . . or else!

Too many of us approach scripture study as just one more thing to check off our to-do list, but studying and searching the scriptures is not a hoop to jump through so that we can earn our place in heaven. The scriptures provide a marvelous blessing and opportunity. Through them we rediscover our heavenly home by learning about our Eternal Father and his son, Jesus Christ. We learn about our spiritual brothers and sisters and how they have kept in touch with home. Most important, we learn that knowledge of our eternal home and family is indispensable if we want to find joy and emerge victorious from this mortal life.

The Savior said that we should "not live by bread alone, but by every word of God" (Luke 4:4). Nephi, too, counseled us to "feast upon the words of Christ" (2 Nephi 32:3). Feasting upon the word of God means more than just nibbling at the banquet table; it involves far more than merely reading. It means developing a love for the scriptures and for studying them.

We all know people who delight in reading the word of God. You can tell by the worn look of their scriptures. I love sitting near a certain BYU religion professor in my ward, because the pages of his scriptures are covered in notes. I doubt there is any white space left in them. Whenever I sit close enough, I try to peek at what he has written and marked because I know he has spent great time and thought in his studies. (Unfortunately, three very active and loudly observant children make it hard for me to peek unobtrusively during sacrament meeting!) I know that he loves reading the scriptures. Like him, we must study eagerly, savoring the truth we find. And the only way to develop this attitude is to start doing it.

Elder Neal A. Maxwell warned:

> There are some among us who have become intellectually weary and who faint in their minds because they are malnourished; they are not partaking regularly of the fulness of the gospel feast. . . .
>
> Spiritual staying power requires strength—strength to be achieved by feasting upon the gospel of Jesus Christ regularly, deeply, and perceptively. If we go unnourished by the gospel feast which God has generously spread before us, we will be vulnerable instead of durable.[10]

Nowhere is the feast of God's word more easily accessible than the books of scripture that are only an arm's length away. Remember that idea that we gain the joy of eternal life by coming to know God? Listen to what Joseph Smith said about the Book of Mormon: "I told the brethren that the Book of Mormon was the most correct of any book on earth, and the keystone of our religion, and a man would get nearer to God by abiding by its precepts, than by any other book."[11]

One of the great things about these letters from home is the layers of meaning in them. Every time we read the scriptures we can find different gems of knowledge that can help us with what we are going through at that time in our life. Our Eternal Father is a master letter writer.

BELIEVE SOMEONE WILL REPLY

When we place a phone call, we always do it believing there is a good chance that someone on the other end will pick up, even if it is voice mail. If we did not believe this, we wouldn't make the call. We have faith that we will be able to contact the person at the other end. Likewise, we need faith in order to stay in touch with our heavenly home.

The dictionary defines faith as "belief that does not rest on logical proof or material evidence."[12] Latter-day Saints believe that faith is to "hope for things which are not seen, which are true" (Alma 32:21). Elder Joseph B. Wirthlin teaches of three components to strong faith: (1) absolute confidence, (2) action, and (3) absolute conformity to God's will.[13] Without all three, our faith is weaker than it could be.

The first component of faith is absolute confidence in God. To have strong confidence in him we must first acknowledge his existence and our relationship to him. Knowing that we are beloved spirit sons and daughters of God is the vital starting point to build faith.

To employ its power, faith must be founded on something reliable. After we know God exists, we need to have a correct idea of his character, which is why the scriptures are filled with numerous revelations and testimonies about God's nature. Today few people have faith in others, and it becomes more and more challenging with all the fraud, lying, and cheating that is rampant in business and society. Astronomically high rates of infidelity and divorce show that many cannot even have faith in their spouse. When we get to know God, we will learn that he is the only thing in which we can have absolute faith, because only he is perfect.

The second component is action. Many confuse faith with belief, but faith is a step further than just belief. Belief is merely agreement or acceptance, while faith impels us to action. James E. Talmage wrote, "One cannot have faith without belief; yet he may believe and still lack faith. Faith is vivified, vitalized, living belief."[14]

The third component of faith is conformity with the will of God. We must earnestly strive to keep the commandments in order to turn the key to the power of faith. John tells us, "If any man will do his will, he shall know of the doctrine" (John 7:17). When we do God's will, then we come to have faith in his doctrine. We can know God's will through the words of scripture and living prophets and in following their counsel we can know we are following God's will. We can pray and listen to the guidance of the Spirit to know that we are in conformity with God's will specifically for us.

Developing and strengthening our faith is a continuous quest. Similar to strengthening our bodies, we have to exercise faith in order to strengthen it. Every time we exercise our faith we will receive confirming evidence by the Spirit, which will fortify our faith. With consistent practice, our faith will become stronger.

Faith has tremendous power. Elder Joseph B. Wirthlin said, "Truly understood and properly practiced, faith is one of the grand and glorious powers of eternity. It is a force powerful beyond our comprehension. . . . Our faith is the foundation upon which all our spiritual lives rest. It should be the most important resource of our lives. Faith is not so much something we believe; faith is something we live."[15]

KEEP CALLING HOME

While we call home through prayer, and come to know our true home while on this earth through scriptures, what implants that knowledge into our hearts and souls so that we will continue to stay in touch is a testimony. "A strong testimony is the unshakable foundation of a secure, meaningful life."[16] A testimony strong enough to be the foundation of our lives can only be obtained through revelation, but we must do some work too. Elder Richard G. Scott said, "Your testimony may begin from acknowledgment that the teachings of the Lord seem reasonable. But it must grow from practicing those laws. Then your own experience will attest to their validity and yield the results promised. That confirmation will not all come at once. A strong testimony comes line upon line, precept upon precept. It requires faith, time, consistent obedience, and a willingness to sacrifice."[17]

In the New Testament we read of a time when the Savior asked his disciples, "Whom do men say that I the Son of man am?" The disciples replied that others speculated that Jesus was one of various prophets, like John the Baptist or Elias. Then Jesus asked the disciples to bear their testimonies: "But whom say ye that I am?"

Only Peter's testimony is recorded. He said, "Thou art the Christ, the Son of the living God." Then the Master replied, "Blessed art thou, Simon Bar-jona: for flesh and blood hath not revealed it unto thee, but my Father which is in heaven" (Matthew 16:13–17).

At this point Peter had received a revelation—he knew that Jesus was the Christ. Some time after this incident, the Savior rebuked Peter, saying, "Simon, Simon, behold, Satan hath desired to have you, that he may sift you as wheat: But I have prayed for thee, that thy faith fail not: and when thou art converted, strengthen thy brethren" (Luke 22:31–32).

President Harold B. Lee reflected on this situation, "Can you imagine the Lord saying this to His chief apostle, to the very man who had previously received a revelation as to the divine mission of the Lord? . . . Peter, somehow, was losing his testimony."[18] However, losing a testimony is not irreversible. Peter did what he needed to strengthen his testimony and become the valiant and strong leader of the early Church.

Unlike acquiring a car or a house, just "getting" a testimony is not the end goal. A testimony is not something that we receive only once. It is an ongoing spiritual witness. As such, a testimony must be continuously nurtured. President Lee also said, "The greatest responsibility that a member of Christ's church has ever had is to become truly converted—and it is just as important to stay converted."[19]

Interestingly, the way to maintain a testimony is nearly identical to how we first gain one. My brother-in-law received great counsel from his mission president before returning home from his mission. His president told him to make sure and do those simple things he had asked investigators to do: read the scriptures, pray, and go to church. If he would do those things, he would keep his testimony vibrant and alive.

These steps apply to those who have had a testimony for years as well as those working to gain one for the first time. We must work through the steps over and over again to strengthen our testimony of the gospel in general or specific doctrines in particular. Harold B. Lee reminded us, "The testimony we have today will not be our testimony of tomorrow. Our testimony is either going to grow and grow until it becomes as the brightness of the sun, or it is going to diminish to nothing, depending on what we do about it."[20]

In times of great trial as well as the times when life just wears us down, we need the strength promised us when we stay in touch with our true home. We need the comfort of our Heavenly Father's love, which is constantly projected through communication with him and through his words. At this time when we are away from home, we need to stay in touch.

I find great joy in the knowledge that I am a daughter of a glorious Heavenly Father who is always available and accessible and who desperately wants me back in his presence. Our loving Eternal Father wants us to reach up to the heavens and touch, if even just briefly, his hand, which is stretched out all the day long (Jacob 5:47). The scriptures express God's love page after page, and I can feel it personally when I approach God in meaningful prayer. Our hearts will lift and we can experience joy when we stay in touch with our true home.

CHAPTER EIGHT STEPS

1. Evaluate your prayers and focus on one thing at a time to improve them. Don't think of this as work; think of it as establishing a better relationship with your Heavenly Father. As you draw closer to him, your prayers will improve.
2. Set aside good time for prayer. If I wait until just before crawling into bed to say my prayers, I know I will rush through because I'm so tired. For me, bedtime is not a good prayer time.
3. Pray more often. Talk to Heavenly Father throughout the day as you would to a friend who is actually there.
4. If you don't feel like praying, then just pray that you will feel like it. When you do not want to pray is usually an indicator that you really need to. Pray until you do feel like it.
5. Ask for the Spirit to help and direct you as you pray. You may be surprised at your own prayers when the Holy Ghost directs them.
6. Pray vocally. It helps you avoid repetition and keeps your mind from wandering.
7. Pray specifically. Don't use generalities.
8. Read the scriptures, looking for information on a topic, rather than like a novel. Keep notes of what you find.

9. As you read the scriptures, try to see them as letters from your Father.

10. Read from the scriptures each day as a family. Set an example for your children. Discuss what you read in simple terms.

11. Remember that the *Ensign* and conference talks in particular are also considered scripture. In fact, the words of living prophets are more valuable than the counsel of ancient ones.

12. Pray for the Lord to strengthen your testimony.

NOTES

1. See Bible Dictionary, "prayer," 752.
2. Joseph B. Wirthlin, "Improving Our Prayers," *Ensign*, Mar. 2004, 24.
3. Gordon B. Hinckley, *Teachings of Gordon B. Hinckley* (Salt Lake City: Deseret Book, 1997), 469.
4. Henry B. Eyring, "Prayer," *Ensign*, Nov. 2001, 15.
5. Clyde J. Williams, "A Shield against Evil," *Ensign*, Jan. 1996, 28.
6. "News of the Church," *Ensign*, Apr. 2000, 74–80.
7. Mike Cannon, "Missionary Theme Was Pervasive during Visit of President Hinckley," *Church News*, Sept. 9, 1995, 4.
8. Ezra Taft Benson, "The Power of the Word," *Ensign*, May 1986, 79.
9. Clyde J. Williams, ed., *Teachings of Harold B. Lee* (Salt Lake City: The Church of Jesus Christ of Latter-day Saints, 2000), 451.
10. Neal A. Maxwell, *Not My Will, But Thine* (Salt Lake City: Bookcraft, 1988), 126.
11. Smith, *History of The Church of Jesus Christ of Latter-day Saints*, 4:461.
12. *The American Heritage Dictionary of the English Language*, 4th ed., "faith," retrieved from dictionary.com, http://dictionary.reference.com.
13. Joseph B. Wirthlin, "Shall He Find Faith on the Earth?" *Ensign*, Nov. 2002, 82.
14. James E. Talmage, *Articles of Faith* (Salt Lake City: Deseret Book, 1984), 87.
15. Joseph B. Wirthlin, "Shall He Find Faith on the Earth?" *Ensign*, Nov. 2002, 82.
16. Richard G. Scott, "The Power of a Strong Testimony," *Ensign*, Nov. 2001, 87.
17. Ibid.
18. Harold B. Lee, *Stand Ye in Holy Places: Selected Sermons and Writings of President Harold B. Lee* (Salt Lake City: Deseret Book, 1975), 91.
19. Ibid.
20. Ibid.

CHAPTER NINE

You've Got to Be Nice

MY THREE-YEAR-OLD DAUGHTER IS unanimously considered a spitfire by our entire extended family. She lets everyone know, in no uncertain terms, exactly what she thinks and feels—and usually at incredible volume. She is also not shy about physically expressing her displeasure. We have worked hard with her on the concept of being nice to others. I know that it is finally starting to click because she now walks around saying, in her sweet little voice, "You got to be nice to people! Don't say stupid! Got to be nice!" or "Don't hit people! Got to be nice!" or "You help people! Got to be nice!"

Positive psychology has concluded that in order to have deeper, more meaningful happiness, "you got to be nice" to people. Dr. Martin Seligman states that one of the big differences between those who feel only somewhat happy and those who feel greater happiness is how much they are involved in activities that are in harmony with a noble purpose; how much they do for the greater good.[1]

Kindness and service to others give you a lift unlike anything else. The boost of joy that comes from service cannot be duplicated through bodily pleasure or induced chemically. We only feel this deep, meaningful happiness when we are developing character through righteous acts. We feel elevated and inspired when we consciously choose to do good. The Lord has told us and now science agrees: serving others makes you happier!

DELIGHT IN SERVICE

Albert Schweitzer once said, "I don't know what your destiny will be, but one thing I do know: the only ones among you who will be really happy are those who have sought and found how to serve."

In the Doctrine and Covenants the Lord commands, "Be not weary in well-doing" (D&C 64:33), and that "men should be anxiously engaged in a good cause" (D&C 58:27). This focus on service is not restricted to our dispensation either. The Lord commanded ancient Israel to "love thy neighbor as thyself" (Leviticus 19:18), and in the Americas, Alma instructed his son to teach the people "to never be weary of good works" (Alma 37:34). Service is an important part of discipleship, because "when ye are in the service of your fellow beings ye are only in the service of your God" (Mosiah 2:17).

Service not only helps those we serve but furnishes an essential component to our own life. It is said that the best way to find yourself is to lose yourself in the service of others. President Spencer W. Kimball further enlightened us with these words:

> It is by serving that we learn to serve. When we are engaged in the service of our fellowmen, not only do our deeds assist them, but we put our own problems in a fresher perspective. When we concern ourselves more with others, there is less time to be concerned with ourselves. In the midst of the miracle of serving, there is the promise of Jesus that by losing ourselves, we find ourselves.
>
> Not only do we "find" ourselves in terms of acknowledging guidance in our lives, but the more we serve our fellowmen in appropriate ways, the more substance there is to our souls. We become more significant individuals as we serve others. We become more substantive as we serve others—indeed, it is easier to "find" ourselves because there is so much more of us to find![2]

Missionaries often end up deeply loving the people and the place where they serve their missions. Why? Missionaries set aside their life for a single purpose: to serve their fellow brothers and sisters. They do service projects, help others, and, above all, they provide an eternal service as they teach others the gospel. As a by-product of this focus on service, missionaries grow personally and learn to love service and those they serve.

Another instance where love is a by-product of service is in the relationship between a parent and child. The first years of a child's life require much sacrifice and service on behalf of the parent, and that service forges a bond of love between them. This bond grows and deepens as the parent continues serving the child through many years.

The goal is to delight in service, for when we merely do it out of obligation we miss the deeper meaning and joy to be found in serving others. Remember, "Tell me and I forget, show me and I remember, involve me and I understand." The way to learn how to love service is to do it. As we serve others and grow to love them, we will feel more delight in doing it and can have greater happiness and joy in our own life as well.

GOD'S HANDS AND FEET

All of us, at times, have reached to God for help. When our needs are great and we plead for aid, the way our loving Heavenly Father most often responds is through his faithful children who love and serve their neighbors. We are God's hands and feet and eyes and ears; he works through us. We are not secondary or subordinate in his work—we are the heart and soul of it.

Recently, it has been an indescribable experience to serve alongside other wonderful people in my ward and neighborhood as we provide considerable assistance to my good friend who I have mentioned before. What I have not mentioned is that she was a divorced mother with three children at home when her son was diagnosed with brain cancer. The diagnosis was unexpected and sudden, requiring immediate hospitalization and surgery.

As this young boy underwent six brain surgeries in the course of three weeks, many people pulled together to take care of the other children, the house and pets, and the dizzying amount of paperwork and errand-running that accompanies a serious illness and extended hospital stay. The collective effort of those involved made it possible for this mother to stay by her son's side.

So far this boy has also gone through intensive and exhaustive chemotherapy and radiation treatment, accompanied by more time in the hospital. The willingness of ward members and neighbors to continue helping this family has never abated, and this mother can count on an army ready to serve her family.

I am profoundly grateful for the chance I have had to learn more about the life-changing blessings of service in this situation. The willingness to serve and love from others has helped my friend and her children realize how much Heavenly Father loves them. And not only has this family been blessed and their faith strengthened through this service, but as a ward we have grown closer and more unified as well. I personally have experienced more joy during this challenging experience than I can even express. I am so grateful to my loving Heavenly Father for allowing me to serve as his hands and feet.

The immediate and severe nature of situations like this one provide ample service opportunities in sporadic bunches, but many serve quietly and diligently all the time. For example, my grandmother has dedicated her time and energy for months to helping the humanitarian effort. She has sewn hundreds of bandages and infant nightgowns, crocheted innumerable hats, and now is making quilts that can be sent wherever they are needed throughout the world. My grandmother does very little else and declares that she will continue to serve in this quiet way the rest of her life.

I want to insert a word of caution here. Although we are mandated to help others, we cannot be all things to all people. We must do all we can, but only as much as we can. Every one of us only has a certain number of gifts we can use to bless others, but when we combine our talents with those that others possess, we then have a full complement of gifts available to everyone. We can each be an instrument in the hands of God, but like the diversity of instruments in an orchestra, we are not all the same one.

Many people served my friend and her family in different ways. Some took care of the pets, some drove the other children where they needed to go, some helped clean house, some brought meals, some coordinated all the efforts, some took care of bills, some stayed at the hospital, and so forth. None of these faithful servants could have done all of these by themselves, but with everyone doing their part we were able to do all that needed to be done. Separately we just had a small part; together we performed a masterpiece. And that is how it is supposed to work.

The most effective and useful types of service occur when we focus enough to clearly define a need and consider how we can truly help fill that need. Real need-based service takes thought and mental effort. Often, those who need our help the most are the last ones to ask for it.

Elder Neal A. Maxwell explains that the sins that keep many saints from reaching their potential are usually sins of omission. He observes that "most omissions occur because we fail to get outside ourselves."[3]

Potential helpers are often simply unaware that help is needed. We are a service-oriented church, but without an awareness of others and their needs, how will we know who, when, and where to serve?

Bishop J. Richard Clarke, formerly of the presiding bishopric, noted, "How many times have we observed a benevolent act performed by someone and asked ourselves, 'Why didn't I think of that?' Those who do the deeds we would have liked to do seem to have mastered the art of awareness. They have formed the habit of being sensitive to the needs of others before they think of themselves."[4] When we can see, recognize, and understand the needs of others, we can render true service—the kind that changes our lives as well as theirs.

I learned one of the best lessons on how to serve from a wonderful neighbor. When my second child was born we immediately ran into serious problems with breast-feeding. It was a battle to feed my baby, and with a high-maintenance first child under two, I was quickly exhausted, frustrated, and constantly on the verge of tears. During that awful first two weeks, my neighbor called and informed me that she was coming to take my toddler for a couple hours, and would ten o'clock or eleven be better?

She didn't ask what she could do to help, or if I would like her to babysit. I have a fiercely independent streak and probably would have turned her down and pretended that things were fine. My neighbor just saw a need and matter-of-factly took care of it. I try to follow her example, and when I see a chance to serve someone, I just do it. So far I have never had someone upset or offended that I didn't ask first, but I know that if I had asked, they might not have let me serve.

We can provide frequent service by simply buying something for someone else or donating money (such as with fast offerings), but sometimes we can't just give money. At these times, it is the giving of ourselves—our personal time and attention—that becomes the service. Spencer W. Kimball said, "To give of oneself is a holy gift."[5] Many acts of service consist of simple encouragement or of giving mundane help with mundane tasks, but "by small and simple things are great things brought to pass" (Alma 37:6).

When we cannot serve directly, or when the need is beyond our power or wisdom, we can still provide service. Sometimes we may not be able to help the person in need, but we can support those who can help. In the situation of the young boy with cancer, many people who were unable to help the family personally offered their service to those who could. For example, several sisters watched my children so I was free to run necessary errands for my friend's family or be with them at the hospital. All those who benefited from this more roundabout way of serving understand that it is invaluable. Just because it wasn't direct service doesn't mean it was any less important.

In these types of situations we can also appeal to God through our faith and prayers. Heartfelt, genuine prayer can mobilize the powers of heaven on behalf of others. An angel appeared to Alma the Younger as a result of prayers from his father and other Church members (Mosiah 27:14). Do not underestimate the power of service through prayer, especially when coupled with fasting.

Service is imperative for true followers of Jesus Christ. The Savior himself lived a life of service, of doing good to all men—friends and enemies alike. We too must develop the same love for people. "Our hearts must go out to them in the pure love of the gospel, in a desire to lift them, to build them up . . . and love them as children of God whom the Lord loves."[6]

In order to become more like Christ we need to feel some measure of his love for others, and we do this through service. As we serve others our love for them will grow. I know that I feel more love for my friend and her family every day as I do things for them, and I can sense further love from the others in our ward. People know when real caring is extended to them; many yearn for it. As the love of men around us waxes cold, our love can and will shine like a light in the darkness.

Sister Mary Ellen Smoot stated, "If we are to be a 'standard for the nations,' we must arise in loving service. . . . As the tide of selfishness sends its waves so high in the world, we can determine to change that tide by being pure vessels of Christlike love and service. Service is the essence of Christ's gospel. Service is the antidote to the ills of our time."[7]

When we follow the Savior's example of service and let the Lord use us as his hands, we will experience deeper, more meaningful happiness. We will feel joy that does not come in any other way. To find this extra sweet joy, "you got to be nice."

CHARITY

The acts of our hands are usually how we serve our fellow man. However, we need to serve God with more than just our might and strength. "He who looks into our hearts and knows our minds demands more than this," says Elder Dallin H. Oaks. "In order to stand blameless before God at the last day, we must also serve him with all our heart and mind. Service with all of our heart and mind is a high challenge for all of us. Such service must be free of selfish ambition. It must be motivated only by the pure love of Christ"[8]

Contrary to the way much of the world views charity, we do not see it as merely giving handouts to others. Mormon connected the word *charity* to the Savior. He declared that "charity is the pure love of Christ, and it endureth forever" (Moroni 7:47). Many scriptures emphasize the importance of charity. Nephi states that "the Lord God hath given a commandment that all men should have charity" (2 Nephi 26:30). Both Nephi and Mormon also state that unless men have charity, they are nothing (2 Nephi 26:30; Moroni 7:44). Why is charity so important?

In answering, I will refer to a talk by Elder C. Max Caldwell of the Seventy. He talks about how the phrase "love of Christ" can have meaning in three dimensions: (1) love *for* Christ; (2) love *from* Christ; and (3) love *like* Christ.[9]

LOVE *FOR* CHRIST

The first dimension of charity is love *for* Christ, when Jesus is the object of our love. Therefore, our lives should be an external expression of our gratitude for him. As we grow in understanding of what our Savior did for us through the Atonement, then our love for him also grows. We not only have gratitude for the overarching effects of the Atonement, but our love for Christ will deepen when we realize the cost to him personally in order to save each of us individually.

Elder Neal A. Maxwell pointed out:

> When the unimaginable burden began to weigh upon Christ, it confirmed His long-held and intellectually clear understanding as to what He must now do. . . . Later, in Gethsemane, the suffering Jesus began to be "sore amazed" (Mark 14:33), or, in the Greek, "awestruck" and "astonished." Imagine, Jehovah, the Creator of this and other worlds, "astonished"! Jesus knew cognitively what He must do, but not experientially. He had never personally known the exquisite and exacting process of an atonement before. Thus, when the agony came in its fulness, it was so much, much worse than even He with his unique intellect had ever imagined![10]

Our love for the Savior—our charity—grows out of the love that the Savior has for us, because, as John taught, "We love him, because he first loved us" (1 John 4:19). We will want to serve the Lord as we gain a fuller realization of what he did for us, and as we serve him that love will continue to grow. Just as a mother's love for her newborn child expands to an unbreakable bond through years of sacrifice and service, our love for Christ will grow in the same way.

LOVE *FROM* CHRIST

The second dimension of charity is love *from* Christ. The prophet Moroni declared, "Thou hast said that thou hast loved the world, even unto the laying down of thy life for the world. . . . This love which thou hast had for the children of men is charity" (Ether 12:33–34). The Atonement was an act of phenomenal love.

By completing the severe requirements of the Atonement, the Savior offered the ultimate expression of love. He taught, "Greater love hath no man than this, that a man lay down his life for his friends" (John 15:13).

Through the Atonement we can feel love from our Heavenly Father as well. By permitting his Son to make such a selfless and suffering sacrifice, the Father provided us with an ultimate expression of his love. "For God so loved the world, that he gave his only begotten Son" (John 3:16).

One of the most memorable and poignant talks on this subject was given by Melvin J. Ballard. Here is how he envisioned our Eternal Father feeling during the Atonement:

> In that hour I think I can see our dear Father behind the veil looking upon these dying struggles until even he could not endure it any longer; and, like the mother who bids farewell to her dying child, has to be taken out of the room, so as not to look upon the last struggles, so he bowed his head, and hid in some part of his universe, his great heart almost breaking for the love that he had for his Son. Oh, in that moment when he might have saved his Son, I thank him and praise him that he did not fail us, for he had not only the love of his Son in mind, but he also had love for us. I rejoice that he did not interfere, and that his love for us made it possible for him to endure to look upon the sufferings of his Son and give him finally to us, our Savior and our Redeemer. Without him, without his sacrifice, we would have remained, and we would never have come glorified into his presence. And so this is what it cost, in part, for our Father in Heaven to give the gift of his Son unto men.[11]

Charity as love *from* Christ is a gift to be received. If we do not receive the Atonement, then we will not be able to dwell with our Father in Heaven. We must receive this gift—this love from Christ—or we will have wasted our purpose for coming here. Even when out of stubbornness or pride we don't receive it, the Savior continues to willingly offer it. He says, "O, ye nations of the earth, how often would I have gathered you together as a hen gathereth her chickens under her wings, but ye would not!" (D&C 43:24). The choice is ultimately ours.

LOVE *LIKE* CHRIST

The third dimension of charity is to love *like* Christ. To love like Christ, charity surpasses just actions, although that is an integral part. As Latter-day Saints, we are striving to develop charity as an attitude, a state of heart and mind. Charity becomes more than just an action. It is an attribute.

If we would truly seek to be more like our Savior and Master, learning to love as he loves should be our highest goal. We can have many virtues, but if we do not also have charity, the others will have little value. Elder C. Max Caldwell stated, "Charity is not just a precept or a principle, nor is it just a word to describe actions or attitudes. Rather, it is an internal condition that must be developed and experienced in order to be understood. We are possessors of charity when it is a part of our nature. People who have charity have a love for the Savior, have received of his love, and love others as he does."[12]

It is not possible to fully love as Christ loves without his help, for pure love cannot be developed solely by exercise. But neither is this love exclusively a gift that requires no effort on our part. Obtaining the pure love of Christ requires both our obedience and Christ's gracious giving. By ourselves, we cannot learn to love with a godlike love, for charity comes "by grace . . . after all we can do" (2 Nephi 25:23) and is "bestowed upon" the "true followers" of Christ (Moroni 7:48).

Loving like Christ does more than influence us to serve others, it is essential in our progression toward eternal glory. Near the end of the Savior's visit to the Americas, he asked, "Therefore, what manner of men ought ye to be?" He then answered the question, "Verily I say unto you, even as I am" (3 Nephi 27:27). By his own instructions we are to become as Christ. Elder Bruce C. Hafen of the Quorum of the Seventy taught, "The purpose of the endowment of charity is not merely to cause Christ's followers to engage in charitable acts toward others, desirable as that is. The ultimate purpose is to transform his followers to become like him."[13]

Charity is so important because it is one of those special principles of the gospel of Jesus Christ that Elder Dallin H. Oaks was referring to when he said, "In contrast to the institutions of the world, which teach us to *know* something, the gospel of Jesus Christ challenges us to *become* something."[14]

THE ULTIMATE EXAMPLE

The Lord told Moses, "For behold, this is my work and my glory—to bring to pass the immortality and eternal life of man" (Moses 1:39). Our Father in Heaven's entire purpose is to provide service, to bring eternal life and happiness to his children. If we do not perform service, then how can we ever hope to be as he is?

Jesus Christ is the ultimate model of service, love, and charity. He came to earth and dedicated his whole life to the service of others. Elder Jeffrey R. Holland reminds us, "True charity, the absolutely pure, perfect love of Christ, has really been known only once in this world—in the form of Christ Himself, the living Son of the living God. As in everything, Christ is the only one who got it all right, did it all perfectly, loved the way we are all to try to love."[15]

Christ told us to do the works which we have seen him do (3 Nephi 27:21) and become like him (3 Nephi 27:27). Luke adds to the Savior's words, "Be ye therefore merciful, as your Father also is merciful" (Luke 6:36), "as if to suggest," comments Elder Holland, "that mercy is at least a beginning synonym for the perfection God has and for which all of us must strive."[16]

Service helps us to get to know the Savior, for "how knoweth a man the master whom he has not served?" (Mosiah 5:13). Devoted service and discipleship are the same. Alma told prospective members at the waters of Mormon that those who are baptized must be "willing to bear one another's burdens," "to mourn with those that mourn," and to "comfort those that stand in need of comfort" (Mosiah 18:8–9).

It is impossible to align our lives with the teachings of Christ and not find opportunities to serve. We will take the initiative, accept and magnify callings, and eagerly engage in good works voluntarily. By choosing to do the Lord's work we become like him.

I am confident that the more we serve, the more we will view the opportunities as a blessing to our lives instead of as a sacrifice of time, talent, or substance for others. We will find joy as we serve others and follow the example of our Savior, who gave himself as a total and unqualified sacrifice for all mankind. Elder Marion G. Romney said, "Service is not something we endure on this earth so we can earn the right to live in the celestial kingdom. Service is the very fiber of which an exalted life in the celestial kingdom is made." [17]

CHAPTER NINE STEPS

1. Smile at those you meet.
2. Read Mosiah 4:6–16. Notice how it is centered on love *for*, love *from*, and love *like* Christ. Pick one of the three dimensions and focus on it for a time. Then focus on another.
3. Make sure to volunteer for opportunities to serve. Put your name on the sign up sheets that go around.
4. Cultivate your awareness of others' needs. Get to know people, and if you have an idea for a way that you can help, be brave and just do it!
5. Keep working on feeling the love of the Lord for you. When you can feel his love, you naturally treat others in a more loving way.
6. Contact those you visit or home teach more often than once a month. Call them or just stop by for a quick chat. They will know you care and you will have more opportunities to serve. It is hard to help when you only see them for thirty minutes a month.
7. When you attend the temple, put the names of those needing assistance from the Lord on the prayer roll. If no temple is close by or you cannot attend for other reason, call the temple and the workers will add the names for you.
8. Instead of asking general questions like "Is there anything I can do to help you?" list specific things you are willing to do. For example, "Can I watch your kids for an hour so you can finish your project?" or "Can I come over this Saturday and help you pull weeds?"

NOTES

1. Seligman, *Authentic Happiness,* 112.
2. Spencer W. Kimball, "Small Acts of Service," *Ensign,* Dec. 1974, 2.
3. Neal A. Maxwell, "Swallowed Up in the Will of the Father," *Ensign,* Nov. 1995, 22.
4. J. Richard Clarke, "Love Extends Beyond Convenience," *Ensign,* Nov. 1981, 79.
5. Spencer W. Kimball, *The Teachings of Spencer W. Kimball* (Salt Lake City: Bookcraft, 1982), 246.
6. Ezra Taft Benson, *Come unto Christ* (Salt Lake City: Deseret Book, 1983), 96.
7. Mary Ellen Smoot, "Arise and Shine Forth," BYU Women's Conference Archive, online at ce.byu.edu/cw/womensconference.
8. Dallin H. Oaks, "Why Do We Serve?" *Ensign,* Nov. 1984, 12.
9. C. Max Caldwell, "Love of Christ," *Ensign,* Nov. 1992, 29.
10. Neal A. Maxwell, "Willing to Submit," *Ensign,* May 1985, 70.
11. Melvin J. Ballard, "Classic Discourses from the General Authorities: The Sacramental Covenant," *New Era,* Jan. 1976, 7.
12. C. Max Caldwell, "Love of Christ," *Ensign,* Nov. 1992, 29.
13. Bruce C. Hafen, "Beauty for Ashes: The Atonement of Jesus Christ," *Ensign,* Apr. 1990, 12.
14. Dallin H. Oaks, "The Challenge to Become," *Ensign,* Nov. 2000, 32.
15. Jeffrey R. Holland, "How Do I Love Thee?" *New Era,* Oct. 2003, 4.
16. Jeffrey R. Holland, "He Hath Filled the Hungry with Good Things," *Ensign,* Nov. 1997, 64.
17. Marion G. Romney, "The Celestial Nature of Self-reliance," *Ensign,* Nov. 1982, 91.

CHAPTER TEN

Protect the Home Front

DOMESTIC DISTURBANCES

There are many sayings that express the important place of the home in our lives. Phrases such as "Home is where the heart is," "Home sweet home," and others assure us that truly, "There's no place like home." Just as a house does not make a home, home is more than just a place. The word *home* makes us think of family and those we love. At the end of our eternal journey, being with our loved ones will be a substantial part of our eternal home and our eternal joy.

Before I continue, let me assure you, as a child who was raised by a single mother, I know the heartache associated with the "imperfect" family. I know that for various reasons many do not have the blessings of intact families or marriages, and may feel uncomfortable or hurt by the emphasis on families in the Church. If this is the case with you, I hope these gentle words of President Spencer W. Kimball provide comfort as this chapter unfolds. He said, "We have no choice . . . but to continue to hold up the ideal of the Latter-day Saint family. The fact that some do not now have the privilege of living in such a family is not reason enough to stop talking about it. We do discuss family life with sensitivity, however, realizing that many . . . do not presently have the privilege of belonging or contributing to such a family. But we cannot set aside this standard because so many other things depend upon it."[1]

Some may feel that because of their situation they do not fall under the umbrella of the Church's definition of family. *Home* and *family*, according to Elder L. Tom Perry, encompasses the lives of the single Latter-day

Saints, single LDS parents and their children, and married Saints who have no children, as well as two-parent homes with children.[2] Thus, we all are part of home and family.

Our belief in the overriding importance of families is rooted in the restored gospel. "The fulness of eternal salvation is a family affair," says Elder Dallin H. Oaks of the Quorum of the Twelve Apostles. He continues, "The gospel plan originated in the council of an eternal family, it is implemented through our earthly families, and has its destiny in our eternal families."[3]

As President Kimball taught, so much depends on the family. "The family is the primary support structure in God's plan to help us resist evil, overcome weakness, and work out our salvation. For this reason we should do all we can to strengthen the family in these days of confusion and opposition."[4]

Unfortunately, too few people hearken to the words of modern-day prophets, seers, and revelators, and the erosion of marriages, families, and homes seems to be growing exponentially. For example, divorce has become an increasingly popular—and easy to obtain—solution to marital difficulties. It is currently projected that approximately 50 percent of married couples in the United States will divorce. The divorce rate for couples in second marriages is even higher, approaching 60 percent. A significant number of married couples in the United States also give divorce serious consideration but then decide to stay married.[5]

My husband is a principal of five hundred elementary students and regularly sees the same turmoil and heartache caused by divorce in the lives of many students. Friendships suffer, learning is negatively impacted, and attendance declines. When the divorce is particularly nasty, he has seen the school ground become a battlefield for the parents in their war for the affection and allegiance of the children.

The family unit seems to be unraveling, and our society appears ever more angry and unhappy. Elder Bruce C. Hafen remarks that "many children, parents, and spouses are turning their hearts not toward one another but toward their own self-focused needs."[6] To an unprecedented degree, the fabric of society is coming apart at the seams as the bonds of kinship and marriage become more and more fragile.

The rising rates of adolescent crime, births to unwed parents, divorce, and family violence reflect some results of this problem. "But the attitudes that produce these statistics," Elder Hafen says, "are in some ways more revealing than the statistics themselves."[7] These social problems are just a by-product of the transformation of our society from one that strengthens the bonds between people to one that is, at best, indifferent to them. More often, these bonds are not seen as uplifting and enriching but as depriving and confining. Nowhere is this shift in viewpoint more obvious than in the attitude toward the institution of marriage.

More and more people view marriage as a couple's relationship, designed to fulfill the emotional needs of adults, rather than as an institution for bringing up children. Many marriages are made and dissolved based on "what's in it for me"—if couples even bother with marriage at all. A growing number of people move in with each other, and then when the going gets hard or boring, they move on, in a vertigo-inducing shift of partners and homes. There is also the growing conviction that any sort of commitment, even just cohabiting, limits personal fulfillment and is therefore undesirable.

We can see this noncommittal mentality toward family extending to children as well. President James E. Faust observed, "Another disturbing challenge to the family is that children are becoming less valued. In many parts of the world, people are having fewer children. Abortion is probably the clearest sign that couples do not want children. An estimated one-quarter of all pregnancies worldwide end by induced abortion."[8]

Not only are children not wanted before they are born, but once they get here there is a disturbing attitude—a new kind of adult disinterest and neglect toward children. In the book *Children without Childhood*, author Marie Winn describes a profound alteration in society's attitude toward children, which she says is connected to many factors. Among these are: a general erosion of institutional authority, a new sense of instability in marriage, the sexual revolution, and the emerging but unjustified tendency to treat children as if they have the capacity for unrestricted adult experience.[9] Children are left on their own with an alarming amount of autonomy, as if parents can't be bothered to guide and direct them. As a result, many children are raising themselves.

Sometimes rather than being uninterested or neglectful of children, adults can instead have an obsession with children's achievements and how that reflects on the parents. The term *trophy child* is often employed when parents use their child to impress other people and enhance their own status. These adults want children to show off to others, and they see the children merely as an extension of themselves. Often their expectations are difficult to fulfill.

As if things aren't confusing enough, some people even argue that parents actually have little influence on their children. In 1998, psychologist Judith Rich Harris published the book *The Nurture Assumption: Why Children Turn Out the Way They Do; Parents Matter Less Than You Think and Peers Matter More,* which argues that after parents contribute an egg and sperm filled with DNA, virtually nothing they do or say makes a difference to what kind of adult their child becomes. Harris contends that peer groups teach children how to behave out in the world, so the best way for parents to shape their children is to make enough money to live in a good neighborhood, buy their children nice clothes, and give them what they need to fit in with the "right" peers.[10]

In contrast, the Lord has always emphasized the essential nature of marriage, family, and home. His prophets through the ages have exhorted people to remember the importance of family. In 1995, the First Presidency issued "The Family: A Proclamation to the World." In bold and unequivocal terms, it champions the importance of the family. It clarifies what a family ought to be and why, cutting through the mists of confusion. Elder M. Russell Ballard says, "The proclamation's clear and simple language stands in stark contrast to the confused and convoluted notions of a society that cannot even agree on a definition of family, let alone supply the help and support parents and families need."[11]

The social sciences are just beginning to see what prophets have been telling us all along. In 2002, the Institute for American Values published a report titled "Why Marriage Matters: Twenty-One Conclusions from the Social Sciences." This report summarized the findings of more than a dozen family scholars and included over ninety-three citations from research and published articles. The report concluded that marriage is an important social good, associated with an impressively broad array of positive outcomes for children and adults alike.[12]

President Ezra Taft Benson taught, "Marriage, home, and family are established by God as part of His divine plan for the blessing of His children. The richest blessings and deepest joys of this life and the life to come are tied up with the performance of these sacred duties. In fact, our very exaltation in the celestial kingdom is directly related to the family and the eternity of the marriage covenant."[13]

The joys of family are not set aside until eternity, though. We can have great joy in our families now. I used to work in a nursing home, and

I quickly learned that most of the elderly people who lived there cared about their families more than anything else. They didn't worry so much about the jobs they had or any of their material possessions, but they cherished their families. All of us, whether married or single, are eternally part of some family. When we recognize and develop those family relationships, we can find much joy in life.

UNDER ATTACK

Since family is a gospel pillar and a potential source of great joy, it is no surprise that the family is under attack from all sides. The adversary understands very well the central role the family plays in the destiny of God's children and has mustered his forces accordingly. Ardeth G. Kapp, former general Young Women president, said, "Today a battle is being waged, and it is no ordinary battle. The safety, the protection, the survival, the sanctity of the family are under attack as never before. The traditional family structure is disintegrating, and many individuals are suffering deep and serious wounds. There is an increasing number of casualties. . . . The enemy is real, and the family is the target."[14]

In ancient America the Lord's people faced a similar desperate battle when they were threatened by enemies both inside their society and out. Captain Moroni lifted up the title of liberty to inspire the Nephites to stand and fight for their freedom and families, and recently the Church leaders have "call[ed] upon members of the Church everywhere to put family first and to identify specific ways to strengthen their individual families."[15] Strengthening families is our sacred duty as parents, children, extended family, leaders, teachers, and individual members of the Church.

As society moves away from marriage, family, and home, it is imperative that we dedicate ourselves to strengthening these areas. It will require hard work to resist the tide. We know that in the end good will conquer evil, but if we as parents (especially mothers) are not home a significant portion of the time, who will be the watchmen on the tower and send up warning cries when evil approaches? I am profoundly grateful that I am around to intervene and teach my children when they are young and first exposed to negative influences.

ON THE FRONT LINE

In the past, the family was considered the "shock absorber" of society. It was the place where individuals, bruised and battered from doing battle with the world, could return to find peace and rest to their souls. However, as the family continues to crack and shatter under the blows of modern life, rather than cushion its members from the harsh realities of life, many families may actually produce an additional measure of trauma. Under the relentless attack of the adversary, many families are simply unable to provide a needed refuge.

We must work to make the home a safe haven for family members, especially as the world outside grows more evil. President James E. Faust said, "As we recall the commandment to stand in holy places, we should remember that beyond the temple, the most sacred and holy places in all the world should be our own dwelling places. Our homes should be committed and dedicated only to holy purposes. In our homes all of the security, the strengthening love, and the sympathetic understanding that we all so desperately need should be found."[16]

Part of making the home a refuge is strengthening families. We must stand strong, even if it comes to the point where we are the only ones defending and fighting for family. We may often feel outnumbered, but we cannot give up, "because so many other things depend on it."[17]

A small line of defense can make a huge difference, as this example from the American Civil War shows. In the summer of 1863, Colonel Joshua Lawrence Chamberlain of the Union Army was given the command of a large group of mutineers to replace the heavy casualties suffered by his regiment. He was instructed to shoot any that refused to fight. Rather than commanding with a heavy hand, however, Colonel Chamberlain treated the men with respect, doing his best to meet their needs, and earned their respect in return.

Within days the Battle of Gettysburg commenced and Colonel Chamberlain received orders to defend and maintain the extreme left flank of the Union line at a small wooded hill known as Little Round Top. If Confederate artillery gained access to the high ground, they could decimate the rest of the Union line. Colonel Chamberlain knew he and his 478 men—almost one-fourth of them had tried to desert the army before—must fulfill their responsibility and hold their ground at all costs.

Confederate commanders also realized the strategic significance of Little Round Top and ordered wave after wave of attacks. After the fifth wave of Rebel soldiers had withdrawn, Chamberlain's defenses remained unbroken but severely damaged. As the Rebel soldiers began to prepare for a sixth assault, the surviving soldiers of Chamberlain's regiment informed him that they had exhausted their ammunition. Chamberlain's bold solution to this desperate situation was to order a bayonet charge, which completely caught the Rebel soldiers by surprise and sent them retreating in panic.

Several days and 50,000 casualties later, the Union had won one of the most decisive engagements of the Civil War. It is widely believed that holding Little Round Top helped turn the tide of the Civil War in favor of the Union, and it forever influenced the course of American history.

Today an unseen yet fierce battle is being waged for the minds, hearts, and even the souls of our family members. We are on the front line of this battle, and we must hold our ground at all costs. We may be outnumbered, but with the Lord on our side the numbers do not matter, "for they that be with us are more than they that be with them" (2 Kings 6:16). A small number of people *can* make a big difference.

STRENGTHENING FAMILIES

Just as the rugged terrain of Little Round Top provided an excellent defense for Chamberlain's small group of soldiers, the Lord needs us to create homes that are fortresses against the rising tide of evil. Our homes are the headquarters for this battle, and it is our charge to be the defenders of the home and family wherever we are.

Captain Moroni was incredibly successful at defending his people against the invading Lamanites who were intent on slaughtering them. The book of Alma contrasts the way that Moroni prepared for war with how his enemy Amalickiah prepared for war. "Now it came to pass that while Amalickiah had thus been obtaining power by fraud and deceit, Moroni, on the other hand, had been preparing the minds of the people to be faithful unto the Lord their God" (Alma 48:7). Moroni spent a great amount of time fortifying and strengthening his people. He fortified them spiritually by helping them increase their faith and by strengthening them physically through training and teaching them how to defend themselves (Alma 48:14–15).

In battle, part of an effective defense is fortifying and strengthening not only your soldiers but also the location you are occupying. Accordingly, not only did Moroni prepare his people, but he also made sure to prepare their cities. He strengthened the Nephite cities so well that the Lamanites were "exceedingly astonished" (Alma 49:9), for the Nephites were prepared for battle "in a manner which never had been known among the children of Lehi. Now they were prepared for the Lamanites, to battle after the manner of the instructions of Moroni" (Alma 49:8). Moroni's preparations were so good, the Lamanites could not overtake the Nephites like they thought they could, and had done in previous engagements. "And thus [Moroni] did fortify and strengthen the land which was possessed by the Nephites" (Alma 48:9).

We can learn a lot from Moroni's strategy (that's why Mormon included the story in his abridgement of the Book of Mormon). We too have an enemy intent on destroying us spiritually, and we too have our homes and families to defend. Like Moroni, we must fortify and strengthen our families, both the individuals in them and the institution itself.

It's been said that the most important thing that a father can do for his children is to love their mother, so a vital part of strengthening families is strengthening marriages. Elder Hugh W. Pinnock of the First Quorum of the Seventy reflected that more marriages would be successful if we devoted the same dedication to them as we often do to a chosen profession, hobby, or home improvement projects. He remarked, "I know of nothing worthwhile in life that comes easy—and nothing in life is as valuable as a strong marriage and a secure family."[18]

Elder Pinnock suggests ten practical things that will fortify a marriage:[19]

1. Bring the Savior and his teachings into your homes and hearts.
2. Do not feel that disagreements in your marriage indicate that it cannot succeed.
3. Never make your mate the object of jokes, either in private or in public.
4. Do not smother each other with excessive restrictions.
5. Compliment each other sincerely and often.
6. Never resort to the silent treatment.
7. Say, "I'm sorry," and really mean it.
8. Never turn to a third party in time of trouble (except appropriate family members, your bishop or stake president, or a counselor).
9. Retain the joy in your marriage.
10. Pray often.

Obviously, as parents we can do many things to strengthen our family. My husband often says that if we don't set the tone in our house, somebody else will—usually referring to Lucifer, be it through TV, music, the Internet, or other negative influences. As the love of men waxes cold, we see many people interact with each other in a rude, disrespectful, and mean manner. If we don't pay close attention, this atmosphere will work its way into our homes. We must strive to set a caring, patient tone in our home, and that requires purposeful effort.

Contrary to what many might believe, Colonel Chamberlain's deed in the Civil War that turned the tide was not the battle of Little Round Top—although that was impressive. The pivotal act happened before Chamberlain's troops ever entered the Battle of Gettysburg. What made the glorious victory at Little Round Top possible were the seemingly small, insignificant acts: caring for the mutineers, listening to them, and treating them with respect. Without the mutineers who stayed and fought beside Chamberlain, the outcome would have been significantly different.

Likewise, the seemingly small, insignificant acts in our homes can make the victory of the family possible. Elder M. Russell Ballard said, "Our family-centered perspective should make Latter-day Saints strive to be the best parents in the world. It should give us enormous respect for our children, who truly are our spiritual siblings, and it should cause us to devote whatever time is necessary to strengthen our families. Indeed, nothing is more critically connected to happiness—both our own and that of our children—than how well we love and support one another within the family."[20]

How do we protect, preserve, and strengthen our families? By following the counsel of the Lord's prophets and giving highest priority to family prayer, family home evening, gospel study and instruction, and wholesome family activities. The First Presidency reminds us, "However worthy and appropriate other demands or activities may be, they must not be permitted to displace the divinely-appointed duties that only parents and families can adequately perform."[21]

One of the best things we can give to our family is time. As I grow older I believe more and more that one of the most precious commodities in life is time. It never stops, and once it is gone it can never be regained, no matter who we are. We have many choices and obligations that take up this valuable commodity, but the most important thing we can do with our time is to strengthen our family members. Taking time can be as simple as eating together, talking together, working together, and playing together.

There are many things we can do to strengthen our own marriages, families, and homes. The question then arises, how can we strengthen the families of others? The truth is that our reach is not limited to our own home. We can also have tremendous influence on others' families.

My mother teaches piano to over thirty students of varying ages. Part of her service is to go to people's homes to teach their children. Over the years she has noticed the influence for good that she can have on her students and their parents through the words she says and how she treats them. She is also an example to the many families who are not members of the Church that she sees every week. Her reach is not limited to her own home.

When we are good home or visiting teachers, we can help bring the Spirit into the homes of those we visit and give them words of encouragement and counsel, which can help them be better parents. At times of stress and crisis we can also help shoulder the burdens of our neighbors and friends so they have more energy to work with their own families. For example, we can clean their house so they can tend a sick relative, cook them dinner so they can be at the hospital with an injured child, or take care of yard work or errands so their time is freed to help their own family.

More indirectly, we can help strengthen the family by being informed voters. We can become aware of current issues and debates and get involved as advocates for the family. Just recently, a letter from the First Presidency was read in sacrament meetings throughout the world encouraging us to support legislation and other community initiatives that reaffirm the sanctity of marriage and family. We know Satan is fighting to destroy families, and we can't let him do it right under our noses.

REJOICE IN PARENTHOOD

Knowing that exaltation is eternal fatherhood and eternal motherhood, Satan's most powerful tactic in his campaign to destroy home and family is to diminish the role of mothers and fathers. Knowing what the Lord—through his prophets—has said about these roles will help us counter Satan's influence and find great joy.

The First Presidency stated, "Motherhood is near to divinity. It is the highest, holiest service to be assumed by mankind. It places her who honors its holy calling and service next to the angels."[22] Yet society advocates the right of women to do more with their life than be "just a mom," as if the role of mother is an underachievement of time and talent. The world today often downplays or even belittles the importance of motherhood.

My husband's mother stayed home to care for her children, and the first time I ever saw my husband angry occurred while we were dating and I inadvertently insulted her. In the course of talking about future plans, I commented that I did not want to be "just a mom." An earnest discussion ensued (more like a heated debate) and I was surprised by the depth of his conviction that our future children have a full-time mother and be privileged to have the same motherly blessings that he deeply cherished. It was clearly a make-or-break issue for him. I finally, yet reluctantly, agreed—partly because I knew the prophets counsel women to stay home with their children and partly because I did not want to lose him. Today I count that as one of the most valuable lessons forced upon me, because, three children later, I know the value in being "just a mom."

There is also tremendous value in being "just a dad." We have already discussed how removing fathers from the home affects our view of and relationship with our Father in Heaven. Elder Jeffrey R. Holland speaks of the book *Fatherless America*, by David Blankenhorn, which studies other repercussions from the loss of fathers: "In this study the author speaks of 'fatherlessness' as 'the most harmful demographic trend of this generation,' the leading cause of damage to children. It is, he is convinced, the engine driving our most urgent social problems, from poverty to crime to adolescent pregnancy to child abuse to domestic violence. Among the principal social issues of our time is the flight of fathers from their children's lives."[23]

Throughout the Savior's ministry we can see the wonderful relationship between Christ and his father. Christ always seemed to be thinking of him, praying to him, and giving all glory and praise to his father. Above all, Jesus' whole purpose in life was to please his father and obey his will.

Elder Holland asks, "As a father, I wonder if I and all other fathers could do more to build a sweeter, stronger relationship with our sons and daughters here on earth. Dads, is it too bold to hope that our children might have some small portion of the feeling for us that the Divine Son felt for His Father? Might we earn more of that love by trying to be more of what God was to His child?"[24]

Children need a mom and a dad, and a home with both is the ideal setting. Unfortunately, we do not live in an ideal world. Many families must do their best with a single parent. They have to rely even more on the Lord to give them strength because they do not have a spouse to assist in caring for the home and children.

Elder Holland also exhorts mothers and fathers to live the gospel as conspicuously as they can because some of the most potent teaching happens through how we live our lives. He warns that even when parents "feel secure in their own minds regarding matters of personal testimony, they can nevertheless make that faith too difficult for their children to detect."[25] And children learn more from what they see than what we say.

Parenting is more challenging than any other role, because, unlike a job or career, it is the only one that will continue forever. While few human challenges are greater than being good parents, few opportunities offer greater potential for joy. President Hinckley asserts, "Of all the joys of life, none other equals that of happy parenthood. Of all the responsibilities with which we struggle, none other is so serious. To rear children in an atmosphere of love, security, and faith is the most rewarding of all challenges. The good result from such efforts becomes life's most satisfying compensation."[26]

It is sometimes easier to remember and focus on the irritating, frustrating, or backbreaking aspects of parenting, and "family bashing" is a popular pastime. But I have found profound happiness and joy in being a mother. When my little girl reaches up and spontaneously kisses me while I help her get dressed and my son tells me he loves me "double never ending," my happiness washes away some of the difficulties. I treasure moments like the time I came upon my three children huddled together on the couch, the oldest reading a picture book out loud while his brother gently played with his younger sister's hair as her head lay in his lap. These moments enlighten my life with a sweet joy that I never would have had if I weren't "just a mom."

CIRCLE THE WAGONS

Years ago, pioneers traveled west across the dangerous American wilderness in large wagon trains. The wagons would travel in a straight single line, resembling a slow-moving train. At night the wagon master would have the wagons form a big circle for protection. Inside the wagon circle was a safe zone, where children would play, adults would cook and take care of the daily chores, and everyone would eat, socialize, and relax. If the train was attacked during the day, they would also circle the wagons as a defensive measure.

Just as a wagon train needed to band together against danger and attack, we need to circle the wagons as Satan and his forces attack home and family. In 2004 the *Ensign* published a year-long series on strengthening the family. In it was this statement: "As Satan and his emissaries work to tear down the family, many people are losing sight of the joys and blessings a strong and loving family can offer. In this gathering gloom, the teachings and ordinances of the restored gospel shine as a unique beacon of hope. As we build our families upon the gospel's firm foundation, our light will shine brighter and attract those who are seeking hope and happiness in a deteriorating world that offers neither."[27]

Stronger marriages, homes, and families will help us be happier, and as we find joy and rejoicing as part of eternal families, we will stand out. We should be a light on a hill; the salt of the earth. As such, it is our responsibility to study, prepare, and work at being articulate enough to teach the truth about our priorities and privileges as members of the Church. We must show the world that we are not apologizing for our emphasis on family and strengthening the home but are rather pursuing our highest priorities—personally, socially, and theologically.

We are on the front line in this war against the family. Just remember that wartime does not mean we cannot be happy and joyful. Captain Moroni lived and led his people through years of war, "but behold there never was a happier time among the people of Nephi, since the days of Nephi, than in the days of Moroni" (Alma 50:23).

I am grateful too for my growing testimony of the importance of marriages, families, and homes. I thank the Lord that I have been sealed in the temple to a husband who regularly compliments, supports, and encourages me. I am humbled by the privilege of being entrusted with the care of three remarkable, noble children. The realization that I am part of an eternal family unit is a thrilling prospect, one that sustains me and prompts me to be just a little more patient, just a little more selfless, and a lot more grateful for the Lord's eternal plan of salvation.

CHAPTER TEN STEPS

1. Set aside time to spend one-on-one with each child.
2. If married, commit to regular date nights.
3. Attend the temple as regularly as possible. Elder Richard H. Winkel told us, "When you come to the temple you will love your family with a deeper love than you have ever felt before. The temple is about families."[28]
4. Treat family members with respect. Never be mean-spirited or provoke your child to anger. Discipline in private, but praise in public.
5. Hold family prayer. There is real meaning behind the oft-quoted adage, "The family that prays together stays together." There is power in family prayer.
6. Hold family home evening regularly, with both lessons and recreational activities. Specific time set aside to discuss spiritual matters is more imperative now than ever before.
7. Read the scriptures as a family. President Hinckley promises that as you read the scriptures, especially the Book of Mormon, "there will come into your lives and into your homes an added measure of the Spirit of the Lord, a strengthened resolution to walk in obedience to His commandments, and a stronger testimony of the living reality of the Son of God."[29]
8. Filter the media that enters your home, just as an officer would filter enemy propaganda that reaches his soldiers.
9. Wives, shower your husbands with affection. Husbands, find little ways to serve your wives every day. Think of your spouse's happiness over your own.
10. In a notebook or a journal write the things you love about each member of your family. Be specific. Then set a time such as birthdays, Thanksgiving, or the beginning of the year to add any especially endearing stories or events. Periodically reread what you have written to help you foster more love for your individual family members.
11. Stand up for home and family. Don't be afraid to be vocal. These days it is becoming almost a fight to do good. Remember you are on the front line.

NOTES

1. Spencer W. Kimball, "Privileges and Responsibilities of Sisters," *Ensign*, Nov. 1978, 101.

2. As summarized in "Follow the Lord's Blueprint for Strong Homes, Families Urged," *Ensign*, Mar. 1986, 83.

3. Dallin H. Oaks, "Parental Leadership in the Family," *Ensign*, June 1985, 7.

4. "Strengthening the Family: The Family Is Central to the Creator's Plan," *Ensign*, Dec. 2004, 50.

5. Brent A. Barlow, "Eternal Marriage Begins in Mortality," *Ensign*, Oct. 2005, 45.

6. Bruce C. Hafen, "Planting Promises in the Hearts of the Children," *Ensign*, June 1994, 46.

7. Ibid.

8. James E. Faust, "Strengthening the Family: Multiply and Replenish the Earth," *Ensign*, Apr. 2005, 18.

9. As quoted in Bruce C. Hafen, "Planting Promises in the Hearts of the Children," *Ensign*, June 1994, 46.

10. Sharon Begley, "The Parent Trap," *Newsweek,* 1998.

11. M. Russell Ballard, "What Matters Most Is What Lasts Longest," *Ensign*, Nov. 2005, 41.

12. Brent A. Barlow, "Eternal Marriage Begins in Mortality," *Ensign*, Oct. 2005, 45.

13. Benson, *The Teachings of Ezra Taft Benson*, 490–91.

14. Ardeth G. Kapp, *My Neighbor, My Sister, My Friend* (Salt Lake City: Deseret Book, 1990), 101.

15. M. Russell Ballard, "What Matters Most Is What Lasts Longest," *Ensign*, Nov. 2005, 41.

16. James E. Faust, "Who Shall Ascend into the Hill of the Lord?" *Ensign*, Aug. 2001, 2.

17. Spencer W. Kimball, "Privileges and Responsibilities of Sisters," *Ensign*, Nov. 1978, 101.

18. Hugh W. Pinnock, "Making a Marriage Work," *Ensign*, Sept. 1981, 33.

19. Ibid.

20. M. Russell Ballard, "What Matters Most Is What Lasts Longest," *Ensign*, Nov. 2005, 41.

21. "Policies, Announcements, and Appointments," *Ensign*, June 1999, 80.

22. First Presidency, in Conference Report, Oct. 1942, 12–13.

23. Jeffrey R. Holland, "The Hands of the Fathers," *Ensign*, May 1999, 14.

24. Ibid.

25. Jeffrey R. Holland, "A Prayer for the Children," *Ensign*, May 2003, 85.

26. Gordon B. Hinckley, "Save the Children," *Ensign*, Nov. 1994, 52.

27. "Strengthening the Family: The Family Is Central to the Creator's Plan," *Ensign*, Dec. 2004, 50.

28. Richard H. Winkel, "The Temple Is about Families," *Ensign*, Nov. 2006, 9.
29. Gordon B. Hinckley, "A Testimony Vibrant and True," *Ensign*, Aug. 2005, 3.

CHAPTER ELEVEN

Be Proud of Peculiar

WHAT DO YOU MEAN, PECULIAR?

In a prophecy regarding our day, Peter identified members of the Church as "a chosen generation, a royal priesthood, an holy nation, a peculiar people" (1 Peter 2:9). Moses also employed the term when he said, "Thou art an holy people unto the Lord thy God, and the Lord hath chosen thee to be a peculiar people unto himself, above all the nations that are upon the earth" (Deuteronomy 14:2).

Most of us feel comfortable, even flattered, to be called *chosen*, *royal*, and *holy* by the Lord. Those words are inspiring and uplifting. But what about *peculiar*? Modern dictionaries define peculiar as "unusual," "odd," or "strange." I know I don't like to be considered strange. What kind of compliment is that?

Elder Russell M. Nelson explains that the term *peculiar* as used in the scriptures is quite different from how we use it today. He said:

> In the Old Testament, the Hebrew term from which peculiar was translated is *segullah*, which means "valued property," or "treasure." In the New Testament, the Greek term from which peculiar was translated is *peripoiesis*, which means "possession," or "an obtaining."
>
> Thus, we see that the scriptural term peculiar signifies "valued treasure," "made" or "selected by God." For us to be identified by servants of the Lord as his peculiar people is a compliment of the highest order.[1]

A peculiar people is one whose relationship to God is out of the ordinary, and thus they are especially valuable. Not only is a peculiar people distinct from all other nations, but that distinction lies in their moral and spiritual excellence. We become the Lord's peculiar people only as we morally and spiritually shine.

As Latter-day Saints, we are peculiar because of our religious beliefs that differ from other Christian creeds and churches. Our practices based on those differences also make us stand out. Even more particular than that, however, is our belief that the gospel must be lived daily and sincerely—that "faith without works is dead" (James 2:20). Our doctrine impacts daily behavior, like what we eat or drink, what we wear, what we do for entertainment, and even what we do or don't do one day a week. A church that makes religion an everyday affair in these days is different indeed.

While I was growing up, I was often oblivious to jokes and practices that were crude and unseemly. Friends who weren't members of the Church teased me good-naturedly about it, and many times would stop others from telling dirty jokes, saying indulgently that I was too innocent, that I just didn't think that way. This and the open knowledge that I didn't drink, fool around, or swear made me stand out from many of my peers.

Another peculiar thing about the Latter-day Saints is our legacy of courage in living up to our beliefs in the face of adverse practices. Elder Widtsoe said, "The world marvels at such daring, but admires it. Men who love truth above all else, who are guided in their lives by the principles of truth and who dare to conform to them, despite temptation or scoffing companions, are the truly honored ones in the minds of saints and sinners. They are the ones the world is hoping and praying for to lead humanity into peace and happiness. But such courage makes of us a peculiar people."[2]

We sing a hymn that pleads, "More holiness give me."[3] In some ways, the search for more holiness is an invitation to become more peculiar. However, the whole is merely the sum of its parts. If we are not peculiar individually, we will not be peculiar collectively either. Do our actions, lifestyles, and interactions with others mark us as different?

You may find that you can become a peculiar person or a peculiar family within your own ward, or maybe a peculiar ward within your own stake. In Matthew chapter 24, the Savior explained that as we get closer to the Second Coming and Satan's dominion grows, even the "very elect" may be deceived. Joseph Smith's translation of that chapter adds the phrase, "who are the elect according to the covenant" (JS—M 1:22). That refers to covenant Church members—the Lord's own peculiar people—who are deceived by the adversary.

Many of the qualities we emphasize in the gospel cause us to stand out because we become increasingly unworldly, but our leaders worry that some saints are uncomfortable standing out and choose to be less peculiar. President Ezra Taft Benson lamented, "Rather than continue a peculiar people, some are priding themselves on how much they are like everybody else, when the world is getting more wicked. . . . As Latter-day Saints, we too have been called out of the world."[4] And that means we will be peculiar.

President Gordon B. Hinckley reassures us, "Of course you are peculiar. If the world continues its present trend, and if you walk in obedience to the doctrines and principles of this church, you may become even more peculiar in the eyes of others."[5] Be proud of being peculiar!

TAKE A STAND

Without a doubt, we face tremendous challenges in these latter days. To survive spiritually we have to resist the increasingly crafty deceptions and temptations of the devil. Elder L. Tom Perry asserts, however, that just resisting is not enough to remain a distinctive people. We must also "mount a counteroffensive against the temptations and teachings of the world."[6] The Lord commands his peculiar people, "Arise and shine forth, that thy light may be a standard for the nations" (D&C 115:5). We must take a stand.

Elder Marion G. Romney explained that we are inevitably led by one or the other of two opposing powers: God or the devil. Our God-given agency gives us the power to choose, but whether or not to choose is not an option.[7] Today many of us are trying to serve two masters: the Lord and the world, or the Lord and our own selfish interests, or the Lord and our recreational choices, and so forth.

Ultimately there are really only two choices: following the Lord or not—and we cannot do both at the same time. The scriptures are very clear: "No man can serve two masters: for either he will hate the one, and love the other; or else he will hold to the one, and despise the other. Ye cannot serve God and mammon" (Matthew 6:24). If you do not actively choose who you will serve, then the choice is made for you by default. As someone once said, "If we do not choose the kingdom of God first, it will make little difference in the long run what we have chosen instead of it."[8]

We must choose whether we will serve our Lord and Savior, Jesus Christ, or follow the gods of indulgence and sin that surround us on every side. The forces of good and evil are dividing, and soon even the fence-sitters will have to come down on one side or the other. The time has come for us to take a stand. Our prophet has issued the challenge "to stand for that which is right and true and good,"[9] and today is the day of decision. Elder Mark E. Peterson asks:

> If we do know what is right, have we the courage to stand up for it, to defend virtue, to declare the validity of our faith, to oppose false teachings, and to fight the unpopular battle? Have we the moral stamina to confront any and all opportunities and thus preserve truth, uphold cleanliness, and defend the cause of God? The time has come when we must take a far more firm and positive stand than ever before. . . . We must bolster our spiritual fortifications, raise the shield which God has given us, and wield the sword of righteousness and faith as all God's servants should.[10]

Do we have the courage to walk out of objectionable movies? Can we stand firm as parents when children want to do things that are wrong, even when everyone else is doing it? Will we turn off the TV or the radio when what is playing is offensive to the Spirit? Are we willing to be regarded as "mean parents" because we hold our children accountable for their actions and teach them that there is a definite right and wrong? Are we brave enough to act upon what we know is right when those around us—even other Church members—aren't? Will we follow the prophet when his counsel goes against the worldly tide? Are we willing to be peculiar? Are we willing to take a stand?

One time my husband and I decided for family home evening to take our three small children to see a kid's movie that was playing at a local theater. As seems to happen often with small children, we were late arriving and the movie was packed. Fortunately, we managed to find enough seats for all of us. Unfortunately, they were near the very front of the theater in the center of a large row, and we had to climb over several people to seat ourselves. After a while the movie content degenerated from plain stupid to crass, vulgar, and downright inappropriate.

My husband and I exchanged looks across the kids' heads. We gathered our belongings (not a low profile affair) and dragged our loudly protesting children out of the row, stepping on toes and falling into other people's laps the whole way. In front of everyone we marched from the front of the theater to the back and out the building. Some might consider that embarrassing, but we chose to take a stand.

We covenant in the waters of baptism to "stand as witnesses of God at all times and in all things, and in all places" (Mosiah 18:9). We cannot hide from our responsibility to be openly on the Lord's side because we will not be a light to the world if we are ashamed to shine. I now regret the moments in my life when I should have taken a stand and didn't, when I should have done more than just not participate; I should have spoken out against it as well.

If we do not take a stand, then we have effectively joined the ranks of the adversary because, as political philosopher Edmund Burke said, "The only thing necessary for the triumph [of evil] is for good men to do nothing." Elder Russell M. Nelson warns us that if the true and righteous people are silent, those who use truth in unrighteousness will prevail. "We must realize that we are at war," he says. "The war began before the world was and will continue. The forces of the adversary are extant upon the earth. All of our virtuous motives, if transmitted only by inertia and timidity, are no match for the resolute wickedness of those who oppose us."[11]

One person that stood firm in his convictions in the face of very real and immediate opposition was Joseph F. Smith. When he was just nineteen years old, Joseph F. Smith was traveling from California to Utah with a small group of Latter-day Saints. As they set up camp one evening, a group of drunken men rode into their camp on horseback. The men had guns, and they threatened to kill any Mormons who came across their path. Joseph F. Smith, who had been gathering wood, boldly approached the fire. One of the drunken men, pointing his pistol at Joseph, said that it was his duty to kill every Mormon he met. He then demanded, "Are you a 'Mormon'?"

Joseph F. Smith looked the ruffian in the eye and answered, "Yes, siree; dyed in the wool; true blue, through and through." Stunned by this wholly unexpected response, the gunman stopped, dropped his hands to his sides, and, after looking incredulously at Joseph for a moment, said in a subdued tone, "Well, you are the d—— pleasantest man I ever met! Shake, young fellow. I am glad to see a fellow stand for his convictions." The drunken men then rode off and did not bother the Saints again.[12]

As the Lord's peculiar people, we must stand up for those things that are of God, and oppose those that would tear down his children. We are not men and women of the world; we are men and women of God. It is not for us to be led by the world; it is for *us* to lead *them*. When we become comfortable with the idea that choosing righteousness will distinguish us from everyone else, we free ourselves from internal conflict and we are able to feel the happiness and joy that come with righteous living.

PECULIAR ARMOR

To take a stand and remain firm against the evil of today, the Lord instructs us to put on "the whole armour of God" (Ephesians 6:13). Furthermore, when we wear the Lord's armor, he tells us to "lift up [our] hearts and rejoice" (D&C 27:15). The armor of God is not your traditional armor. In fact, you could call it peculiar armor: a shield of faith, a sword of the Spirit, a helmet of salvation, a girding of your loins (meaning "to prepare oneself for something requiring readiness, strength, or endurance"[13]) with truth, and a breastplate of righteousness (D&C 27:15–18).

The last two qualities—truth and righteousness—are of significant importance. I love how the Young Women motto and the Relief Society declaration both proclaim that members of the Church should stand for truth and righteousness.

The scriptures tell us that truth is "knowledge of things as they are, and as they were, and as they are to come" (D&C 93:24). Divine truth is eternal, absolute, and unchanging. Our stance that truth is permanent is peculiar in a time where the concept of truth is becoming more and more flexible. Many see truth as relative, or individual; truth is what you think it is. In contrast, we know truth itself is fixed, but what does change is our understanding of it as we grow in wisdom, knowledge, and spiritual vision. So it is *we* who change, not truth.

The Holy Ghost is the conduit for imparting truth from God to his children, and through him we can "know the truth of all things" (Moroni 10:5). Our Heavenly Father wants to share truths with us, until eventually we know all things (D&C 93:28), but he will only give us knowledge of truth as fast as we are able to receive it. In rare cases the Lord will reveal truth incredibly fast, as with Alma and King Lamoni. For them, the extreme intensity of the instruction knocked them unconscious. Usually, however, the Lord will enlighten us gradually, line upon line.

Truth is more than just an abstract, philosophical concept. It has glory and power, as the Savior revealed, "If ye continue in my word, then are ye my disciples indeed; And ye shall know the truth, and the truth shall make you free" (John 8:31–32). Truth literally frees us from the bondage of ignorance. As we progress spiritually, we learn to accept truth, love it, and find joy in it.

We will also be peculiar as we stand for righteousness. Saints of God are urged to do "the works of righteousness" (D&C 59:23) and to "bring to pass much righteousness" (D&C 58:27). Those who want to live the gospel are usually trying to be more righteous. However, some struggle with understanding exactly what being righteous means. They may mistakenly believe that to be righteous is to be without sin; that righteousness is synonymous with perfection. If righteousness is perfection, then we would all be unable to do as the Lord commanded.

The adversary will even use our efforts to be more righteous against us if we let him. At times in my life I have fallen into the snare of thinking righteousness equaled perfection (or something close to it). I thought I would be happier once I was righteous, like righteousness was a destination and everything would be rosy once I arrived there. This view is not only incorrect, but it can also be discouraging, because we will always stumble in this life. We will always need to repent.

This erroneous view of righteousness can also limit us. The Pharisees and Sadducees worked hard at being righteous. They focused on it so much that they looked beyond the mark and concentrated on every little behavior, rather than on their Lord and Savior.

The best definition I have found of righteousness as we Latter-day Saints view it is "a condition in which a person is moving toward the Lord, yearning for godliness, continuously repenting of sins, and striving honestly to know and love God and to follow the principles and ordinances of the gospel."[14] Righteousness, therefore, is the process of coming unto Christ.

Even with a more correct understanding of what righteousness is, the exact method of how to achieve it is more ambiguous. In the *Ensign* article "Journey toward Righteousness," A. Lynn Scoresby shares his quest to better understand how to become more righteous.[15] He spent much of his life thinking that being righteous meant simply fulfilling all of his church duties, like a checklist of activities. How many of us have a list of things we are supposed to do, like read the scriptures, say a prayer, go to church, and have family home evening, which we perform mostly so we can check them off?

Righteousness, however, is not merely completing a checklist of duties. After recognizing this, Scoresby next adopted the belief that being righteous meant the absence of sin, only to realize eventually that he had missed the mark again. We can only have limited progress in our quest for righteousness if our focus is only on not doing bad things.

Once there was a woman who entered a flower garden contest. She worked and worked and worked on her garden every day, making sure even the tiniest weed was eradicated. She watched the other contestants, secure that she was working harder and longer than any of them. Her flowers bloomed in orderly bunches, with rich, weed-free dirt between them.

Certain that she would easily win the contest, this woman was dismayed when another winner was announced. She complained to the judge, explaining the tremendous time and work that she had put into her garden, more than any of the other contestants. The judge replied that it was not enough to keep pulling all the weeds to keep her garden beautiful. The gardener had to fill their garden so full of flowers there wasn't any room for the weeds in the first place.

People who are trying to overcome addiction are told that they cannot merely stop the harmful behavior. An essential part of triumphing over their addiction is replacing the addictive behavior with productive behavior. Just stopping the addictive behavior will never be enough, because it leaves a void. Addicts must fill that void in order to be successful in avoiding relapses.

In a way, we could consider ourselves addicted to the natural man and worldly pursuits. LDS scholar Robert L. Millet explains:

> Simply stated, the natural man is the man who remains in his fallen condition; he has not experienced a rebirth. At the one end of the spectrum, the natural man may be a person bent on lasciviousness; he may be one who loves Satan more than God and thereby is carnal, sensual, and devilish (see Moses 5:13). . . . At the other end of the spectrum, the natural man may well be a "nice man," a moral and upright person bent upon benevolence. Such a person, acclimated to the present fallen world, still does not enjoy the enlivening powers of the Holy Ghost and does not enjoy the sanctifying power of Christ's covenants and ordinances. Even though the light of Christ is making an impact on him, he has not followed it into the Lord's full gospel truths.[16]

We know we must put off the natural man (Mosiah 3:19), but Elder Neal A. Maxwell points out, "Just as Jesus warned that some evil spirits would come out only with 'prayer and fasting' (Matt. 17:21), the 'natural man' does not come off without difficulty either."[17] Simply put, we cannot be righteous through our own sheer will, the Lord's assistance is required.

Over time, Scoresby discovered that true righteousness was learning about and becoming like God. He realized that he was wrong in trying to *not do* things instead of trying *to do* things. Instead of defining his sins, he should have been defining those attributes he wanted to have. Just like with those overcoming addictions, the most effective way to righteousness is to replace carnal attitudes and habits with godlike ones. The journey to righteousness is really the journey of becoming more like God.

We are all somewhere on that same path of discovery to what righteousness really means and how to become righteous. Righteousness is not a destination. Neither is it something we make ourselves do, like lifting weights, only expecting to enjoy the final results. Neither is righteous living merely how we avoid being penalized. When we choose righteousness because we want to draw closer to God and live righteously to have joy instead of just to avoid punishment, a greater measure of joy is exactly what we will get.

OUR DEFENSE

Righteous living not only brings us joy, but it is also a defense. We are to take upon us the armor of God as a protection against the evil one (Ephesians 6:11–17; D&C 27:15–18). For those of you who might be a little behind in your armor jargon, a breastplate covers your chest and stomach. It is an essential piece of armor because it protects your vital organs. The breastplate guards your heart, so it isn't surprising that the Lord's armor contains a breastplate of righteousness. Our desires come from our hearts, and righteousness protects us from Satan's flaxen cords, which are nearly unnoticeable until they combine into strong cords, which bind us forever (2 Nephi 26:22).

Father Lehi pled with his sons shortly before his death with these words: "Awake, my sons; put on the armor of righteousness. Shake off the chains with which ye are bound, and come forth out of obscurity, and arise from the dust" (2 Nephi 1:23). The armor of God helps deflect behaviors that, if allowed to persist, will turn into debilitating habits.

English writer Samuel Johnson wisely shared, "The chains of habit are too small to be felt until they are too strong to be broken."[18]

Just as iniquitous habits bind us, righteous habits can bind the devil. President Joseph F. Smith taught, "The more righteous and upright, pure and undefiled, the Latter-day Saints become, the less power will Satan have over them, for in proportion to your unity and uprightness, honesty, and fidelity to the cause in which you are engaged, in such proportion will the power of the adversary be weakened."[19]

Nephi teaches that Satan will eventually be bound during the Millennium because of the righteousness of the people (1 Nephi 22:26). This does not mean that power is withdrawn from Satan. Elder Bruce R. McConkie clarifies that Satan will not be bound because men *cannot* sin, but because they *do not* sin.[20]

As we put on the breastplate of righteousness and take a stand for it as the Lord's peculiar people, we will also receive blessings of peace. "But learn that he who doeth the works of righteousness shall receive his reward, even peace in this world, and eternal life in the world to come" (D&C 59:23). As events unfold leading up to the Savior's Second Coming, peace will be harder and harder to find.

Elder William R. Bradford, of the Seventy, said:

> As the forces of good and evil polarize more and more, those who have not prescribed a moral consequence to their actions will find their lives in such chaos that their style of life will be unbearable to them. . . . When that day comes, the righteous Saints of God will be the only well-governed people unto whom the world can turn. It will be there and there only that they will find stability and steadfastness. They will come, not knowing the doctrine of the righteous, but it will be as foretold, "For, behold, I say unto you that Zion shall flourish, and the glory of the Lord shall be upon her; And she shall be an ensign unto the people, and there shall come unto her out of every nation under heaven" (D&C 64:41–42).[21]

President Spencer W. Kimball said to be righteous is a glorious thing in any age, but to be righteous "during the winding-up scenes on this earth, before the second coming of our Savior, is an especially noble calling. The righteous woman's strength and influence today can be tenfold what it might be in more tranquil times."[22]

Righteousness is the better way, and, ultimately, it is the only way. Only in truth and righteousness can we find the joy, happiness, safety, and security that men and women have longed for and searched for through all time. In righteousness we find the exhilaration and joy of being children of God.

As we take a stand, and strive to be more righteous ourselves, our excitement for the things of God will grow. We can be liberated with truth and protected by the Lord's armor. We can be proud to stand out and proud to be peculiar as we echo Paul, who said, "For I am not ashamed of the gospel of Christ" (Romans 1:16).

CHAPTER ELEVEN STEPS

1. Wear your peculiarity proudly. We celebrate and laud being different from society. Be proud that you are different as you follow God.

2. Resolve to take a stand. Decide now that you will speak up when something is wrong. You do not need to be offensive or mean to do this. Remember the occasion when Spencer W. Kimball spoke up. He said, "In the hospital one day I was wheeled out of the operating room by an attendant who stumbled, and there issued from his angry lips vicious cursing with a combination of the names of the Savior. Even half-conscious, I recoiled and implored: 'Please! Please! That is my Lord whose names you revile.' There was a deathly silence, then a subdued voice whispered, 'I am sorry.' "[23]

3. Have the courage to walk away from anything that does not please the Lord.

4. Stand as a witness in the important silent ways: how you dress, what you view as entertainment, and so forth.

5. Write notes, make phone calls, or in person give sincere praise to those around you, especially the youth, who you witness taking a stand for truth and righteousness. You will find joy in the process and the recipient will find encouragement and resolve.

6. Make a list of virtues, strengths, or characteristics you would like to have that would bring you closer to God. Work on a virtue a week as you progress in righteousness. Over time these virtues will become more and more part of who you are.

7. Conduct a family home evening or lesson on being the Lord's peculiar people. Explain that it is a good thing, and that we *will* stick out if we do not follow the trends of the world. Help your kids feel comfortable with it, and as you help them, you will feel better about it too.

NOTES

1. Russell M. Nelson, "Children of the Covenant," *Ensign*, May 1995, 32.
2. John A. Widtsoe, "I Have a Question," *Ensign*, Apr. 1988, 50.
3. "More Holiness Give Me," *Hymns*, no. 131.
4. Benson, *The Teachings of Ezra Taft Benson*, 329–30.
5. Gordon B. Hinckley, "A Chosen Generation," *Ensign*, May 1992, 69.
6. L. Tom Perry, *Living with Enthusiasm* (Salt Lake City: Deseret Book, 1996), 65.
7. As quoted in James E. Faust, "Serving the Lord and Resisting the Devil," *Ensign*, Sept. 1995, 2.
8. Dallin H. Oaks, "Focus and Priorities," *Ensign*, May 2001, 82.
9. Gordon B. Hinckley, " 'True to the Faith,' " *Ensign*, June 1996, 4.
10. Mark E. Petersen, "Where Do We Stand?" *Ensign*, May 1980, 68.
11. Russell M. Nelson, "Truth—and More," *Ensign*, Jan. 1986, 69.
12. Joseph Fielding Smith, *Life of Joseph F. Smith* (Salt Lake City: Deseret Book, 1938), 188–89.
13. *The American Heritage Dictionary of the English Language*, "loins."
14. Daniel H. Ludlow, ed., *The Encyclopedia of Mormonism* (New York: Macmillan Publishing, 1992), "righteousness," 3:1236.
15. A. Lynn Scoresby, "Journey toward Righteousness," *Ensign*, Jan. 1980, 53.
16. Robert L. Millet, "Putting Off the Natural Man: 'An Enemy to God,' " *Ensign*, June 1992, 7.
17. Neal A. Maxwell, "Put Off the Natural Man, and Come Off Conqueror," *Ensign,* Nov. 1990, 14.
18. As quoted in Marvin J. Ashton, " 'Shake Off the Chains with Which Ye Are Bound,' " *Ensign*, Nov. 1986, 13.
19. Joseph F. Smith, in Conference Report, Oct. 1911.
20. Bruce R. McConkie, *The Millennial Messiah* (Salt Lake City: Deseret Book, 1982), 668–69.
21. William R. Bradford, "Righteousness," *Ensign*, Nov. 1999, 85.
22. Spencer W. Kimball, *My Beloved Sisters* (Salt Lake City: Deseret Book, 1979), 15.
23. Spencer W. Kimball, "President Kimball Speaks Out on Profanity," *Ensign*, Feb. 1981, 3.

CHAPTER TWELVE

Two Is Better Than One

THE HOLY PRIESTHOOD OR POLITICALLY CORRECT?

Many people today are concerned with equality. Laws are passed, rallies are staged, and speeches are made extolling its virtues. Although total equality sounds good in theory, in practice it falls far short of the ideal. Most people do not like the idea of having the rewards of their hard work doled out to those who haven't earned it. Communist and socialist regimes try to keep people equal, and the last half a century has seen these governments topple like dominoes. Rather than *equality*, when everyone is the same, most people prefer the idea of *equity*, when everyone has access to the same opportunities. Equity means being just, impartial, and fair.

At the forefront of equality movements for many years is the fight to equalize treatment of women and men. Interestingly, proponents often work toward this equality by driving a wedge between the genders. This is not just coincidence. Satan understands the power wielded by righteous men and women who are united; therefore, he works to confuse us about our natures and stewardships. We are bombarded by baffling, misleading, and even damaging messages about gender, marriage, family, and all male-female relationships.

Our Father in Heaven knew what he was doing when he created us. He did not intend there to be equality of gender (we could never be exactly the same, anyway), but there *is* equity. The divine roles of men and women are different, but one is not more important than the other.

Neither man nor woman is perfect or complete without the other, and neither is dominant over the other.

Women are given the responsibilities of motherhood and sisterhood, and men are given the responsibilities of fatherhood and priesthood. Men and women have complementary, not competing, responsibilities. "Neither Adam with his priesthood nor Eve with her motherhood could bring about the Fall alone. Their unique roles were interconnected."[1] There is difference between men and women, but not inequity.

Elder Neal A. Maxwell stated:

> We know so little . . . about the reasons for the division of duties between womanhood and manhood as well as between motherhood and priesthood. These were divinely determined in another time and another place. We are accustomed to focusing on the men of God because theirs is the priesthood and leadership line. But paralleling that authority line is a stream of righteous influence reflecting the remarkable women of God who have existed in all ages and dispensations, including our own. . . .
>
> Just as certain men were foreordained from before the foundations of the world, so were certain women appointed to certain tasks. Divine design—not chance—brought Mary forward to be the mother of Jesus. The boy prophet, Joseph Smith, was blessed not only with a great father but also with a superb mother, Lucy Mack, who influenced a whole dispensation.[2]

Those who feel the division of roles in the Church is unfair are confusing equality with equity. It is essential that men and women work together as partners, in spite of their differences, in order to fulfill the Lord's purposes. Sheri Dew states, "No marriage or family, no ward or stake is likely to reach its full potential until husbands and wives, mothers and fathers, men and women work together in unity of purpose, respecting and relying upon each other's strengths."[3]

There are those who would have women believe that somehow they are inferior in the Church because they do not hold the priesthood like men; that it is not fair that women cannot preside. It is even likely that a number of women at one time or another have told themselves, "If I can juggle housework, chauffeur kids all over town, magnify my church calling, fend off solicitors, do yard work, supervise homework, mediate arguments, and cook and serve breakfast, lunch, and dinner on time, why can I not be trusted to conduct sacrament meeting?" While feminist advocates have used public pressure to convince other religions to alter their doctrines concerning women clergy, the true Church of Jesus Christ remains peculiar and recognizes the divine differences and responsibilities of gender.

Women in our Church are not oppressed because they are not allowed to have the priesthood because, in truth, women *do* preside. They preside over the lives of their children rather than over an organization, and there are many days that my three children give me all the presiding I need! Unfortunately, with the importance of family in society dwindling, those of the world may see presiding over a family as a lesser role. However, we know better and must keep our eternal perspective.

Most agree that two is usually better than one, and that goes for men and women as well. The Father himself declared that "it is not good that the man should be alone" (Genesis 2:18) and made a help meet for Adam. Eve had her own distinct personality, her own strengths and unique gifts that balanced and complemented Adam's. Together they shouldered the burdens of mortality, followed the commandments of God, raised children, and found joy, for "neither is the man without the woman, neither the woman without the man, in the Lord" (1 Corinthians 11:11).

PRIESTHOOD BLESSINGS FOR ALL

The priesthood is the power of God delegated to man, by which man can act in the earth for the salvation of the human family.[4] Priesthood is divine authority and divine power. "It is the power by which the cosmos was ordered, universes and worlds were organized, and the elements in all their varied structures and relationships were put into place. Through the priesthood, God governs all things."[5] Since priesthood is the means through which God administers his will on earth and heaven, the priesthood will likewise be the vehicle we use to eventually become like him and inherit his joy, glory, and dominion.

Without the priesthood, the earth would be a much different place. In fact, we call much of the period when the fulness of the gospel was no longer on the earth the Dark Ages. Life was hard; people were oppressed; disease, illness, and famine swept across the land; and violence reigned. Written records were few, and advances in technology, literature, art, science, and so forth were practically at a standstill. In contrast, since the late 1800s, which is when priesthood was restored to the Earth, there has been an explosion of change, advancements in every area, and the general quality of human life has improved remarkably.

Thankfully we have the fulness of the priesthood on earth today, and, like all things godly, it is orderly and intentional. And just like the restoration resolved centuries of questions about the nature and character of God, two priesthood principles, when considered prayerfully, can help us more fully understand it.

First of all, the Lord has assigned to men the chief responsibility for the governing and presiding over the affairs of the Church and the family through the priesthood. However, they are to use this sacred power to bless and benefit all members of the Church—men, women, and children.

The blessings essential for growth, progress, and salvation are made available to all through the priesthood: the blessings of being baptized, receiving the Holy Ghost, renewing our covenants through taking the sacrament, and making and keeping temple covenants. Through the priesthood we have access to more joy, and through it all the righteous can also have protection against the powers of darkness. When properly exercised, the priesthood is a great blessing from God to all of his children, because it brings more light, life, and love to this earth and all its inhabitants—past, present, and future.

Second, the fulness of the priesthood contained in the highest ordinances of the house of the Lord can only be received by a man and woman together. President Harold B. Lee said, "Pure womanhood plus priesthood means exaltation. But womanhood without priesthood, or priesthood without pure womanhood doesn't spell exaltation."[6] Priesthood is the power of God, but in order to wield it like God, a man must be sealed to a woman.

Misunderstandings about sacred things are not surprising, especially today, when a staggering number of children grow up without a righteous priesthood leader in the home. Without exposure to how the priesthood works and blesses others, it is easy for these children to misunderstand the proper role of the priesthood in their lives. Young men may not learn to honor it and young women may not learn to recognize young men who do. In this case, two negatives do not make a positive, and young couples may be easily enticed to make poor decisions that have eternal ramifications.

As one of those who grew up without a priesthood leader in the home, I have also felt the effects of a faulty understanding of my place in the priesthood. Fortunately, I had kind home teachers and Church leaders who looked out for me and helped me avoid some of the deeper pitfalls in life. But without a father in the home, I seldom had the opportunity to experience the everyday benefits from the priesthood. It wasn't that I deliberately chose not to; it's just that it was never around.

Even now, after ten years of marriage to a faithful priesthood holder, I still rarely think of asking for blessings for myself. I have no problem requesting them for one of my children, but it often takes a gentle reminder from my husband when I am going through a particularly rough time that I can ask for a blessing. I continue to work on the feeling that the priesthood can be a very real force in my own life. We don't want potential priesthood energy in our home that is waiting to be used. We want kinetic priesthood energy that flows freely and invigorates everything around it.

Women do not hold the priesthood, but they can have great influence on priesthood holders. They can support and encourage husbands, fathers, brothers, and sons in fulfilling their priesthood responsibilities and can also strengthen other priesthood bearers. Young women in particular exert a powerful influence on the younger priesthood holders. By their dress and manner, young women who are modest can help young men keep their eyes and thoughts away from dangerous paths.

The Lord's purposes cannot be fulfilled unless faithful men who bear the priesthood and righteous women who rejoice in serving under the direction of the priesthood can work together. The Lord must have righteous women as well as righteous men to build his kingdom. It takes two.

SUSTAINING THE PRIESTHOOD

We all—men and women alike—have the responsibility to sustain the priesthood. The word *sustain* means to support from below, to uphold as valid, and to confirm or corroborate.[7] The act of raising your right hand to sustain should be much more than rote ritual or a tradition devoid of personal thought and introspection. It is a sacred and solemn responsibility with accompanying spiritual blessings.

Sustaining our Church leaders may seem a little thing, and just raising our hand is a small movement, but what it signifies is of great import. The practice of sustaining Church officers is actually a time of making and renewing covenants. Raising one's hand in a sustaining vote is an outward symbol or token of a significant covenant to which we are agreeing and binding ourselves.[8] When we perceive common consent as a personal covenant, we no longer focus on the person for whom we are "voting" but, rather, on ourselves and our willingness to sustain them.

When we sustain officers, our behavior should show it. We sustain by avoiding criticism of the Lord's anointed leaders—at the local or general level—and by praying for them. We sustain by participating in the programs they direct and by doing what they ask without murmuring or complaining. We also sustain by helping them magnify their callings. Most significantly, we sustain our leaders by following their counsel, and when we have problems with counsel it is up to *us* to fix the problem. We are responsible to know through the confirmation of the Spirit that what and who we are asked to sustain is the mind and will of the Lord.

It can sometimes be hard to see how our act of sustaining priesthood authorities can possibly matter very much, but it really does. As we sustain the priesthood we will be sustained by its power to someday qualify us for all our Father has to give, including godly joy.

PROPHETS

One of the greatest things our Eternal Father has given us through the priesthood is the access to prophets, seers, and revelators who serve as his personal spokesmen. The Lord tells us, "Whether by mine own voice or by the voice of my servants, it is the same" (D&C 1:38). He continues, "He that receiveth my servants receiveth me; And he that receiveth me receiveth my Father; And he that receiveth my Father receiveth my Father's kingdom; therefore all that my Father hath shall be given unto him" (D&C 84:36–38). We need to ask: how are we receiving the Lord's servants?

A prominent theme of the Book of Mormon is that people seldom follow the Lord's servants when living conditions are comfortable, easy, and prosperous. During these periods, people ignore God, reject his prophets, and become distracted from their goal to obtain immortality and eternal life. They search for pleasure, diversion, and status, forgetting the true sources of happiness. From the rebellion of Laman and Lemuel to the fall of Moroni's people, the Book of Mormon is replete with examples of those who ignored the counsel of their living prophets. The result was a "ripening in iniquity" until the inhabitants were destroyed by civil war or natural disasters.

Moroni saw our day in vision when his people, much like Ether's, were gone. He felt impressed to point out parallels between the Nephites, the Jaredites, and the latter-day inhabitants of the promised land. He pleaded, "Repent, and not continue in your iniquities until the fulness come, that ye may not bring down the fulness of the wrath of God upon you as the inhabitants of the land have hitherto done" (Ether 2:11). Will we follow the counsel of God's prophets any better than the former inhabitants did? If we are not wiser than they were, we will suffer their same fate.

The Book of Mormon also abounds in examples of the happiness of the ancient American inhabitants when they did listen to and follow their priesthood leaders. King Benjamin's people, the people of Ammon, and those that followed Captain Moroni all had great measures of joy and happiness. The greatest example is the two hundred years of peace and joy after Christ showed himself to the Nephites. Through the scriptures we see numerous examples that sustaining and following the Lord's prophets leads to joy and happiness, and not following the prophet leads to pride, contention, and unhappiness.

I am profoundly grateful for the priesthood power that has given us prophets who are leading us through a veritable spiritual minefield. As I look back in my life, I can see how the Lord steered a naïve but obedient little girl away from a multitude of potentially disastrous situations. It is only now that I have my own children that I understand how close I could have come to making major mistakes if it weren't for my simple testimony and trust in prophets. I now feel a little like Adam in that when the Lord tells me to do something through his prophet, I don't immediately need to know why (Moses 5:6). If the prophet tells me to turn left, then I'm going to turn left because he knows where the mines are. And I have peace and joy in that faith and knowledge.

THE PATRIARCHAL ORDER

Women know that they can be blessed by the priesthood even though they do not hold it. They also know that they can influence, support, and sustain priesthood leaders. But what is women's place in the priesthood? Are women merely the supporting cast or backstage crew to make sure the priesthood is able to do what it is supposed to?

Yes and no. Women often do play a supporting role to the men in their lives who are exercising their priesthood. Men holding challenging and time-consuming church callings know they would be unable to do it without a supportive wife. However, I believe that many women—and men—misunderstand some vital knowledge about the priesthood and women's place in it.

I say this as a woman who was raised as a Latter-day Saint, who attended Brigham Young University and the required religion classes, who regularly goes to church, who tries to read the scriptures consistently, and who also goes to the temple. Yet until recently I never considered a key aspect about my place in the priesthood of the Lord, and I suspect that many priesthood holders may not have considered it either. It concerns the patriarchal order bestowed upon couples during temple sealings.

We learn from a revelation to the Prophet Joseph Smith that the sealing ordinance, which eternally unites man and woman, is a requirement for exaltation. Without it we cannot live with our Heavenly Father and Jesus Christ in the highest degree of the celestial kingdom, where the power for eternal families is present. Without the sealing ordinance, priesthood power is incomplete.

That revelation, found in section 131 of the Doctrine and Covenants, reads, "In the celestial glory there are three heavens or degrees; And in order to obtain the highest, a man must enter into this order of the priesthood (meaning the new and everlasting covenant of marriage); And if he does not, he cannot obtain it. He may enter into the other, but that is the end of his kingdom; he cannot have an increase" (D&C 131:1–4).

Many people read this section of the Doctrine and Covenants and do not grasp its full import. I know that I did not. It does not merely mean that the presence of a spouse is required to enter the highest degree of glory. We must do more than just present a marriage certificate to gain entry. Yet that is how many people view it.

During the Apostasy the priesthood was taken from the earth; therefore, the Prophet Joseph Smith had to receive it by angelic visitation in order to restore the true Church of God. John the Baptist appeared to restore the keys to the Aaronic Priesthood in 1829. A month later, Peter, James, and John restored the keys to the Melchizedek Priesthood. So which element of the priesthood was the Lord referring to in section 2 of the Doctrine and Covenants when he said:

> Behold, I will reveal unto you the Priesthood, by the hand of Elijah
> the prophet, before the coming of the great and dreadful day of the Lord.

And he shall plant in the hearts of the children the promises made to the fathers, and the hearts of the children shall turn to their fathers.

If it were not so, the whole earth would be utterly wasted at his coming. (D&C 2:1–3)

To answer this question I will refer to the teachings of Ezra Taft Benson.[9] He explained that although there are two *priesthoods* in the Church, the Aaronic and the Melchizedek, there are three *orders* of the priesthood. The lowest is the Levitical or Aaronic order. Then there is the order of Melchizedek. The highest order of the priesthood is the patriarchal order.

Elder Cree-L Kofford of the Quorum of the Seventy helps clarify more about the patriarchal order: "The gospel, which is called 'the new and everlasting covenant,' includes many specific covenants, one being called 'the new and everlasting covenant of marriage.' This title, or name, is simply another way of saying 'patriarchal order.' Thus, that portion of section 131 could read, 'And in order to obtain the highest, a man must enter into the patriarchal order of the priesthood.' "[10]

It was imperative then that Elijah visit the prophet Joseph Smith because he held the keys of the authority to administer *in all the ordinances* of the priesthood, or the sealing power of the patriarchal order. According to Joseph Smith, Elijah was the last prophet to hold these keys of the priesthood, or "the revelations, ordinances, oracles, powers and endowments of the *fulness of the Melchizedek Priesthood.*"[11] The translated Elijah restored these keys to Peter, James, and John on the Mount of Transfiguration. But within a few years came the Apostasy, and the blessings of the fulness of the priesthood were removed from the earth.

In order for this most sacred and powerful order of the priesthood to be restored, the Lord commanded the Saints to build a temple in which it would be administered. "For there [was] not a place found on earth that he may come to and restore again that which was lost . . . *even the fulness of the priesthood*" (D&C 124:28; emphasis added). For this purpose the Kirtland Temple was completed at great sacrifice to the Saints, and Elijah appeared there on April 3, 1836.

The patriarchal order refers to governing priesthood power held by a couple that has entered into the new and everlasting covenant. "This order was instituted in the days of Adam, and came down by lineage . . . that his posterity should be the chosen of the Lord, and that they should be preserved unto the end of the earth" (D&C 107:41–42). It includes the ordinances and blessings of the fulness of the priesthood shared by husbands and wives who are sealed in the temple.

Only in the Lord's house can we enter into the highest order of the priesthood, which will entitle us to all that the Father hath, if we are faithful. It is so wonderful that every modern-day prophet has urged us to make temple attendance a priority. The blessings of temple attendance are many, but it is essential that we go to enter into this highest order of the priesthood, else "the whole earth would be utterly wasted" (D&C 2:3).

The Lord has told us that the patriarchal order will be the order of things in the highest degree of the celestial kingdom, and it can only be held jointly, by both husband and wife. Of course, some may not have the opportunity to marry in this life, but they are promised they will have that opportunity.[12] They must have the opportunity because women are more than just a supporting cast. They are an essential half to the highest priesthood order. But just as men cannot achieve exaltation without women, women cannot without men.

It is so important that we understand our place in the priesthood; we are irreplaceable—both men and women. We can only receive a fulness of joy together. Two is not only better than one—two is essential.

UNITED WE STAND

Although men and women are inherently different, the Lord's plan unites them in power through the patriarchal order. The make-up of our Church is also varied, with members from different backgrounds, economic groups, cultures, and languages—sometimes all in the same ward! This diversity could potentially divide us, but just as couples are to stand jointly in defense of truth and righteousness, the Lord intends that all of his saints stand together as well.

Unity is an important aspect of Godhood, as evidenced when Christ declared, "I and my Father are one" (John 10:30). George Q. Cannon elaborated, "While they [Jesus Christ and Heavenly Father] are two Personages, they are but one—one in feeling, one in thought, one in mind, one in everything, in fact, in every direction in which their power is or can be exercised."[13]

Christ also said of those who would be part of his Church, "Be one; and if ye are not one ye are not mine" (D&C 38:27). The aim has always been unity, oneness, and equality among the members of the Church of Christ, despite what is happening in the world around them. The people of Enoch are shining examples of disciples that were able to reach a state of unity in adverse conditions because at their time in history, the rest of the world was at war.

We read in the book of Moses:

> And there went forth a curse upon all people that fought against God;
>
> And from that time forth there were wars and bloodshed among them; but the Lord came and dwelt with his people, and they dwelt in righteousness. . . .
>
> And the Lord called his people Zion, because they were of one heart and one mind, and dwelt in righteousness; and there was no poor among them. (Moses 7:15–18)

Like the people of Enoch, we too can be unified in the middle of evil and chaos. In fact, righteous unity is imperative to move the work of God forward in such times. Marion G. Romney explained:

> The power of the Church for good in the world depends upon the extent to which we, the members thereof, observe this principle [of unity]. . . .
>
> Surely we need this unity and this strength in this day in which we live. . . .
>
> Only a united people, keeping God's commands, can expect the protection which he alone can give when the floods come, and the rains descend, and the winds blow, and beat upon our house.[14]

I have witnessed the power of unified members as numerous families in the various wards I have lived in have faced severe challenges requiring outside help. Relief Society sisters have responded amazingly to meet the avalanche of needs, providing hundreds of meals, running dozens of errands, babysitting others' children, and joyfully serving countless hours despite inconvenience to themselves. Brethren gave priesthood blessings, shoveled driveways, mowed lawns, planted trees and flowers, and donated their skills by installing new flooring, fixing plumbing, and providing computer technical support. Invariably, in those times where we have worked together in service and love, we have felt an increase of goodness and power.

I have never felt, however, such a strong bond of kinship as I have in my current ward. In addition to the young boy with cancer, there have been many trials we have braved together, and we have not only felt an increase of charity through these experiences, but many have found new joy as well. I liked going to church before, but now I feel a different happiness in being there. As we have sacrificed, worked, and served together for shared goals, we have found a commonality among all of us. We are no longer just a group of people who meet together once a week because we live in our ward's boundaries, and then go home to grow and progress separately. Now there is a feeling that we are a large extended family who are in this together.

As such, we love each other, help each other, lift each other, and sometimes even carry each other along the gospel path to progress. The key is we do it together. I feel like I am a member of a team, and I look at my ward members and know that no matter what happens, I have my team with me. That is a unity that I have never experienced before, and it is precious to my soul.

I am so grateful that the fulness of the priesthood, with its accompanying temple blessings, has been restored to the earth. I am thrilled to know that the priesthood my husband holds and that my sons will hold can be traced back through time to Joseph Smith, Peter, James, John, and ultimately Christ. I am humbled to better understand the unity of the Lord, to be linked to my neighbors and to my husband. It gives me great peace to know that if I am faithful to my temple covenants, someday I can be welcomed home to a fulness of joy with my beloved spirit brothers and sisters and stand hand in hand with my husband to jointly wield priesthood power in the creation of our own worlds without end. And that is great cause for rejoicing.

Two truly is better than one, but when we stand united, we become as one, "of one heart and one mind" (Moses 7:18). The Lord would unite us—men with women, ward members with each other, and eternal brothers and sisters across the globe. When we stand together, unified, we can do so much good. Together we can move mountains. Together we can find joy.

CHAPTER TWELVE STEPS

1. Think about the covenant you make when sustaining others to church callings. Do your best to sustain with future action, not just with your arm.
2. Magnify your own callings.

3. Ask for priesthood blessings when needed. Give priesthood bearers the opportunity to use it.

4. Express appreciation to priesthood leaders for being worthy to hold the priesthood and exercise it in your behalf. Bishops and quorum leaders, for example, exercise priesthood in behalf of other priesthood holders.

5. Research your (or your husband's) priesthood lineage. It is a great feeling to be able to trace your priesthood authority back to Joseph Smith and on to Jesus Christ himself.

6. If married, work on the unity between you and your spouse. Concentrate on working together, consulting each other about family issues and decisions, and doing things together. To foster unity, share goals and time together.

7. Reach out to others in your ward. Get to know them and serve them. You are in this together.

8. Know that you are part of a team. Treat others that way.

NOTES

1. Sheri L. Dew, "It Is Not Good for Man or Woman to Be Alone," *Ensign*, Nov. 2001, 12.
2. Neal A. Maxwell, "The Women of God," *Ensign*, May 1978, 10–11.
3. Sheri L. Dew, "It Is Not Good for Man or Woman to Be Alone," 12.
4. Smith, *Gospel Doctrine*, 139.
5. Ludlow, *Encyclopedia of Mormonism*, "priesthood," 3:1134.
6. Williams, *The Teachings of Harold B. Lee*, 292.
7. *The American Heritage Dictionary of the English Language*, "sustain."
8. Brent L. Top, Larry E. Dahl, and Walter D. Bowen, *Follow the Living Prophets* (Salt Lake City: Bookcraft, 1993), 100.
9. Ezra Taft Benson, "What I Hope You Will Teach Your Children about the Temple," *Ensign*, Aug. 1985, 6.
10. Cree-L Kofford, "Marriage in the Lord's Way, Part One," *Ensign*, June 1998, 7.
11. As quoted in Ezra Taft Benson, "What I Hope You Will Teach Your Children about the Temple," *Ensign*, Aug. 1985, 6.
12. Williams, *The Teachings of Harold B. Lee*, 256–57.
13. George Q. Cannon and Jerreld L. Newquist, comp., *Gospel Truth: Discourses and Writings of President George Q. Cannon, First Counselor to Presidents John Taylor, Wilford Woodruff, and Lorenzo Snow (1880–1901)* (Salt Lake City: Zion's Book Store, 1957), 1:161.
14. Marion G. Romney, "Unity," *Ensign*, May 1983, 17.

CHAPTER THIRTEEN

Reach for Your Destiny

AIM HIGH

When children are asked what they want to be when they grow up, you often hear responses like, "A rock star," "A football player," or "The president." Children believe anything is possible; they always aim high and never dream of mediocrity. You won't hear a child say, "I think I'll stick to digging ditches" or "I want a job that just pays minimum wage."

Prophets throughout time and even the Lord himself urge us to become as a child (Mosiah 3:18; Matthew 18:3). Being childlike is spiritually beneficial because, among other things, children have an optimistic desire to reach for pinnacles of success. The loftiest and most meaningful of all successes is attaining celestial glory. President Wilford Woodruff said, "Celestial glory is worth all we possess; if it calls for every dollar we own and our lives into the bargain, if we obtain an entrance into the celestial kingdom of God it will amply repay us."[1]

When runners enter a race, they do not aim for third place, they all try to be the first across the finish line. We, likewise, should aim for the winner's prize. We did not choose to come here to merely get to the telestial kingdom. We chose to come to Earth so that we could become like our Heavenly Father and return to live with him. We not only chose it, we fought for it. It was worth fighting for in the premortal life and it's worth fighting for now. Our goal is only the very best—our goal is eternal life.

Psychological research on achievement motivation has suggested two motives for doing things: the motive to succeed and the motive to avoid failure. A person with a high motive to succeed strives to achieve a goal because of the positive feelings that come from having achieved it. A person with a high motive to avoid failure is more worried about not failing than actually succeeding, and sometimes there is so much anxiety about failing that he or she does not even try.[2]

Therefore, a person with a high spiritual motive to succeed may have a love of righteousness and strive to achieve spiritual goals because he/she loves the Lord and his commandments. Conversely, a person with a high spiritual motive to avoid failure may also have a desire to live the commandments, but more from fear of the punishments of hell than for the positive attraction to the rewards of heaven.[3]

Do we attend our church meetings because we want to, or because if we don't the Lord may withhold blessings? Do we serve others because we love them, or because we have been told to do so? Do we read our scriptures because our souls feel nourished by the word of God, or because we should read every day? Do we try to come closer to God so that we can become like him, or just do what he tells us to because we know we will not get a good reward if we don't?

Spiritually speaking, too many are motivated more by the fear of failure than the desire to succeed, like avoiding sin rather than developing spirituality. If this attitude persists, many may miss the ultimate goal of celestial glory. Even if failure avoidance managed to land some in the celestial kingdom, I suspect they would feel uncomfortable associating with others who, in every respect, thirsted for righteousness, pursued meaningful service, and sought after all things virtuous.

Regardless of the motive, we will be happier if we obey God's commandments than if we do not. But that happiness will be greater if we are motivated to do so by love of virtue rather than by fear of punishment. The right attitude and vision will help us rejoice as we grow spiritually, instead of just doing it because we ought to and waiting for joy at the end of the journey.

A PATTERN FOR SUCCESS

Of all the children through the ages who have dreamed of greatness —like Michael Jordan, Sally Ride, J. K. Rowling, and Thomas Edison— those who did achieve their high objectives had some things in common: the potential or talent, the right training, the self-confidence to succeed, and the perseverance to consistently work hard to get there. These elements are also essential for us to achieve the eternal greatness we strive for.

The Potential

While only a handful of people have the natural athletic potential to experience the same high-flying success as Michael Jordan, we all have the spiritual potential to become like God. As his children, we are gods in embryo and we have been endowed with every faculty necessary to become like him. For eons before we came to this earth, we were privileged to be in his presence. We knew what kind of being he is, we saw his glory, and desired to be like him.

You are sent to this earth not merely to make a living, have a good time, achieve worldly success, or to satisfy urges, passions, or desires. You are sent here to become as God is and know the joy he knows, and this can only be accomplished through a mortal experience. In this profound sense, joy and happiness arise from what we experience here: pain and grief along with pleasure and enjoyment, responsibility, service, and all other things necessary for personal growth. At the center of God's plan to make maximum joy accessible to his children is the Atonement of Christ.

The Training

Just as Sally Ride (and every other astronaut) underwent years of exhausting physical and mental preparation in order to accomplish her goal of momentarily leaving the confines of this planet, we must also receive tutelage from on high in order to ascend to our heavenly glory. The gospel of Jesus Christ is the curriculum designed to help us achieve our goal, church is the school, and life is the laboratory and practical exam. All three elements work together to provide the proper training for eternal greatness. We must take what we learn at church, in the scriptures, and from the Lord's spokesmen and apply it to our daily lives in order to pass a series of tests that move us forward in our eternal progression. We do not pass the practical exam if we merely go to church and listen to the lessons, only to put them from our mind as soon as we leave.

In James we are told, "But be ye doers of the word, and not hearers only" (James 1:22). My mother knows a woman who is a "doer of the word." She was not able to have much of an education, but she maximizes what she does have. She really listens to the lessons and talks at church and tries hard to apply and implement what is taught into her life. Through their friendship over the years, my mother has been impressed with the personal and spiritual growth of this woman, because she exemplifies the admonition in James to not just hear, but to do.

In the book of Helaman we read the story of Nephi, a great prophet and missionary who retreats to a tower in his garden to mourn the wickedness of his people. As he is praying, a crowd gathers to wonder at his grief. Nephi notices, and then, as a prophet of God, calls them to repentance. The crowd not only heard Nephi's powerful words but received a strong witness of his prophetic powers as he correctly prophesied the death of their chief judge, as well as the murderer's identity.

You would think after this magnificent experience that many would want to hear more of what Nephi could teach them in order to change their lives. Instead, we read, "And it came to pass that there arose a division among the people, insomuch that they divided hither and thither and went their ways, leaving Nephi alone, as he was standing in the midst of them" (Helaman 10:1). The people just left, still debating about who Nephi really was.

Likewise, if you just read the scriptures, conference talks, or even this book and never apply the insights to your life, they will do little to help you. The Lord gives us all the training we require to return back to him, and who could ask for a better coach? The real question is, what kind of pupil will you and I be?

The Self-Confidence to Succeed

As spirit children of God, we received our first lessons in the spirit world, and were prepared to come to Earth. We were among the "noble and great ones" (D&C 138:55) who "shouted for joy" (Job 38:7) at the creation of the Earth because we would be given a physical body with the opportunity to be proven in a mortal sphere. Men and women wanted to work side by side to accomplish eternal goals that neither can attain independently.

We fought for this opportunity because we knew that the Lord would help us and extend as much mercy as possible to us in the end. Reflect back on Moses' encounter with Satan. Moses knew who he was and was confident in his standing with the Lord. Nephi trusted in the Lord to provide a way to get the brass plates and then confidently strode into Jerusalem. Moses and Nephi had self-confidence in their eternal identity and their eternal worth.

As the mother of several children, the wife of an educator, and as an author myself, the Harry Potter phenomenon created by J. K. Rowling has a prominent place in our home. Beyond the enjoyment of the books lies a truly motivating story of a down-on-her-luck single mother who pictured her story published long before any manuscript was even reviewed by a publisher. That vision carried her through eight publisher rejections until her dream was finally realized. Similarly, we need to visualize our glorious destiny and see ourselves through the Father's eyes. If we can believe it, as children of God, we can achieve it.

The Perseverance to Work Hard

"Perseverance is a positive, active characteristic. It is not idly, passively waiting and hoping for some good thing to happen."[4] Perseverance is constantly, consistently striving and energetically struggling for a goal. When we strive for exaltation we don't merely do the minimum amount of work necessary to squeak by; we labor at it every day, all the time. And when we have a setback, we get up, push ahead, and recommit ourselves. It is through this hard work that we become celestial material.

Napoleon said, "Victory belongs to the most persevering." There is no doubt that Thomas Edison understood the principal of perseverance. The appropriate filament material that made the light bulb possible was only discovered after hundreds of failed attempts. This tenacious "stick-to-it-ness" is vital for all athletes, businessmen, parents, politicians, and especially Saints who desire to fight the good fight. Successful victory over the trials of mortality and the natural man is a marathon, not a sprint. We must work hard, come unto Christ, and then endure to the end in order to earn the saving grace of our Redeemer.

BREAK THE CHAINS

Lehi beseeched, "O that ye would awake; awake from a deep sleep, yea, even from the sleep of hell, and shake off the awful chains by which ye are bound, which are the chains which bind the children of men, that they are carried away captive down to the eternal gulf of misery and woe" (2 Nephi 1:13). The chains Lehi speaks of are not made of metal, but they weigh us down, restrict our progress, and bind us just as effectively.

We cannot aim high if we are being dragged down by chains that we have allowed to bind us. If you think about it, anything that pulls us off the path of our eternal destiny chains us down and holds us captive. These chains can make us forget who we are, destroy our self-image, put our family life in jeopardy, hinder our ability to serve our fellow men and our God, and distort our vision of our eternal destiny.

Not only can we allow Satan's heavy chains to keep us back, but sometimes we can be bound and not even realize it. For example, too much preoccupation with worldly things can bind our attention so that there is little room for spiritual matters. Dwelling on the bad things that happen around the world can tie up our emotions so that we fail to notice the blessings of the Lord. And always noticing the negative things about others can fetter our mind so that we forget that they are beloved children of God and our brothers and sisters.

Who among us has not been bound by the chains of unhappiness, poor choices, or bad habits? Have you ever felt the heavy chains of discouragement, low self-worth, or lack of self-discipline? Do you feel the weight of anger, bitterness, or betrayal? These and other chains drag us into misery and woe; they hold us back from drawing closer to God. Alma warned us to beware the snares of the adversary, "which he has laid to catch this people, that he might bring you into subjection unto him, that he might encircle you about with his chains, that he might chain you down to everlasting destruction, according to the power of his captivity" (Alma 12:6). Elder H. Ross Workman remarked:

> Many think of captivity only in terms of imprisonment by other people. Physical captivity is abhorrent, but the effects may not endure eternally. The greater bondage is to the father of lies—a form of captivity that is far more devastating and potentially longer lasting. . . . One can be in captivity to sin or to the pursuit of worldly honors such as fame, wealth, political power, or social standing. One can also be in captivity through obsessive preoccupation with activities such as sports, music, or entertainment.[5]

Freedom to choose is a gift given by God to his children. Accordingly, we can choose liberty and eternal life through Christ, or we can choose captivity and death according to the power of the devil (2 Nephi 2:27). How, then, do we shake off the awful chains of spiritual captivity? Only through our Heavenly Father's plan and our Savior Jesus Christ, who successfully broke the chains of sin and death.

I echo Lehi in saying, "Shake off your chains!" Realize that Heavenly Father's plan is one of happiness and joy, and when you follow it his way, you can find a measure of his joy. Throw off Satan's cords that bind you and reach for your eternal destiny.

OUR DIVINE DESTINY

President Thomas S. Monson once said, "Work without vision is drudgery. Vision without work is dreaming. Work coupled with vision is destiny."[6] Understanding our divine destiny and potential is vital to the successful eternal completion of our lives here on earth. Our spirits yearn for us to remember the truth about who we are, because the way we see ourselves affects everything we do. Satan knows this and attempts to cloud our understanding of how the Lord sees us.

What we are now is not what we can one day become. We are just in the process of becoming what we will ultimately be. Without clear vision of our divine mission and potential, it becomes easier to settle for the diversions and fleeting pleasures of the world. Our destiny is not to have the best job or to lose ten pounds. We will fall short of the ultimate goal if we neglect spiritual matters, even if our houses are beautifully decorated. In the eternities our looks and our careers will mean nothing, and even having the most amazing children will not matter if we cannot be with them. The more clearly we understand our divine destiny the easier it is to resist the enticements of the devil.

When we live according to our eternal vision as God's children, we can begin to truly receive his image in our countenances (Alma 5:14). It is vital that we demonstrate that there is joy in living the way the prophets have told us to live—and if you do live that way you *will* find joy. As Alma taught his son, restoration is not "to take a thing of a natural state and place it in an unnatural state, or to place it in a state opposite to its nature" (Alma 41:12). Those that are clean will be clean still. Those that are happy will be happy still. And those that rejoice will rejoice still.

Our destiny is to be spiritually reborn sons and daughters of God and one day become like our Eternal Father, with all his knowledge, love, and glory. We must understand and remember why we are here and who we really are. Sheri L. Dew asks:

> Will you seek to remember, with the help of the Holy Ghost, who you are and who you have always been? Will you remember that you stood by our Savior without flinching despite the most difficult of opposition? Will you remember that you were reserved for now because you would have the courage and the determination to face the world at its worst and to help raise and lead a chosen generation? Will you remember the covenants you have made and the power they carry? Will you remember that you are noble and great and a potential heir of all our Father has? Will you remember that you are the [son or] daughter of the King?[7]

WILL YOU REMEMBER YOUR DIVINE DESTINY?

The Lord's plan is the pathway to joy. Find it, walk it, and stay on it. We are supposed to have joy in the journey, not just at the end of it. I believe that following the steps outlined in this book can help you learn more about your divine destiny and imprint that knowledge upon your soul. I believe this because it happened to me as I prepared for, researched, wrote, and rewrote this book.

Believe that you are a beloved child of God. Understand that you are meant to have joy, now and in the future. Realize that your life has great purpose. Organize your life and priorities to fulfill that purpose. Choose to have the Holy Ghost as your constant companion. Stay in touch with your heavenly home. Love and serve others. Guard and protect home and family. Stand tall and don't be afraid to stand out. Unite under the priesthood banner of God. Know your divine destiny and don't settle for less.

Then look forward to the day when the Lord shall look at you with love in his eyes, and with open arms will say, "Well done, thou good and faithful servant: thou hast been faithful over a few things, I will make thee ruler over many things: enter thou into the joy of thy lord" (Matthew 25:21). May God bless you and help you enjoy the journey.

NOTES

1. Calkin, ed., *Journal of Discourses*, 17:270.
2. Kenneth L. Higbee, "Achieving Spiritual Goals—Why?" *Ensign*, Nov. 1971, 18–19.
3. Ibid.
4. Joseph B. Wirthlin, "Never Give Up," *Ensign*, Nov. 1987, 9.
5. H. Ross Workman, "Breaking the Chains of Sin," *Ensign*, July 2006, 52.
6. As quoted in Benson, *Teachings of Ezra Taft Benson*, 200–201.
7. Sheri L. Dew, *No Doubt About It* (Salt Lake City: Deseret Book, 2001), 53–54.

About the Authors

JAIME THELER

Jaime Theler grew up in Colorado. She graduated from Brigham Young University with a bachelor's degree in physical therapy. Jaime has written one other book, also co-authored with her mother, *Parenting the Ephraim's Child: Characteristics, Capabilities, and Challenges of Children Who Are Intensely MORE*. Jaime now lives in American Fork, Utah, and has three children.

DEBORAH TALMADGE

Deborah is a native of western Colorado. She studied both piano performance and geology at Mesa State College in Grand Junction, Colorado. She has studied under piano masters in the United States and Italy and now teaches private piano lessons around her writing schedule. In addition to co-authoring *Parenting the Ephraim's Child* with her daughter Jaime, Deborah has written two fiction novels, *The Apprentice* and *The Heldan*. She is the mother of three and the grandmother of five.

0 26575 08397 2